100
GREATEST TRIPS

TRAVEL
+LEISURE

100
GREATEST TRIPS

FROM THE EDITORS OF THE WORLD'S
LEADING TRAVEL MAGAZINE

2008 EDITION

TRAVEL
+LEISURE
BOOKS

AMERICAN EXPRESS PUBLISHING CORPORATION
NEW YORK

TRAVEL + LEISURE
100 GREATEST TRIPS 2008 EDITION

Editors Laura Begley, Nina Willdorf
Project Editor Melinda Page
Assistant Managing Editor Meeghan Truelove
Art Director Sandra Garcia
Reporters Tom Beer, Andrea Bennett, Mario Lopez-Cordero, Carolina A. Miranda, Bunny Wong
Photo Editors James Owens, Nicole Schilit
Copy Editors Stephen Clair, Brad Engelstein, Mike Iveson, Margaret Nussey, Shazdeh Omari, Kathy Roberson
Production Editor David Richey
Researchers Catesby Holmes, Elyse Lightman, Aimée Lutkin, Shavanna Miller, Mary Staub
Assistant Book Editor Bree Sposato
Editorial Assistants Christine Ajudua, Tanvi Chheda
Proofreader Susan Groarke
Interns Kyle Dyer, Julia Houlihan

TRAVEL + LEISURE

Editor-in-Chief Nancy Novogrod
Creative Director Nora Sheehan
Executive Editor Jennifer Barr
Managing Editor Michael S. Cain
Arts/Research Editor Mario R. Mercado
Copy Chief Jane Halsey
Photo Editor Katie Dunn
Production Manager Ayad Sinawi
Editorial Business Associate Andrew G. Forester

AMERICAN EXPRESS PUBLISHING CORPORATION

Senior Vice President, Chief Marketing Officer Mark V. Stanich
Vice President, Books and Products Marshall Corey
Senior Marketing Manager Bruce Spanier
Assistant Marketing Manager Sarah Ross
Corporate Production Manager Stuart Handelman
Senior Operations Manager Phil Black
Business Manager Tom Noonan

Cover design by Sandra Garcia
Cover photograph by Max Kim-Bee
Page 9: The infinity pool at
Clos Apalta Winery, in Chile.
Opposite: The courtyard of the Riad
Dar Al Batoul, in Rabat, Morocco.

ISBN 1-932624-27-9
ISSN 1933-1231

Published by American Express Publishing Corporation
1120 Avenue of the Americas, New York, New York 10036

Distributed by DK Publishing, Inc.
375 Hudson Street, New York, New York 10014

Manufactured in the United States of America

CONTENTS

INTRODUCTION

BY NANCY NOVOGROD, EDITOR-IN-CHIEF

First, my definition of a trip that's great enough to be included in this volume: one that transports you beyond the geographic boundaries of a destination and gives you the opportunity to immerse yourself in the here and now—while transcending the everyday. In short, a travel experience that changes you and alters your perception of the world. For this, the second book in T+L's annual series *100 Greatest Trips*, we chose a collection of stories from the past 12 months that represents most fully our world-wide range of destinations, with travel ideas that span the price scale and a universe of tastes.

To simplify your navigation of the world, and these pages, we've organized our trips by continents, countries, cities, and regions. And in our final section, The Guide, we offer maps, addresses, and brief descriptions of the locations covered, in order to make the process easier still. The passions of today's travelers are highlighted throughout: tasting the exemplary Rieslings and Sauvignon Blancs of Hungary and the Cabernet-Merlot blends of New Zealand's Waiheke Island; finding the most in-the-know spots for dining on local specialties in Manhattan, Provence, and Guangzhou; and shopping for cutting-edge home accessories in Amsterdam, diamonds in Antwerp, and the latest looks in Los Angeles. For the adventurous, there's a family itinerary to Vietnam, a contemporary-art tour of Cairo, and a hiking trip in Patagonia. And for beach lovers, there are ample stretches of sand in Belize, Italy's Le Marche, and Fiji.

A common thread runs throughout the disparate journeys: the quest for intimate one-of-a-kind experiences that teach you and transform you by taking you beyond your familiar boundaries. These sorts of memorable interludes are laid before you in every issue of the magazine. At *Travel + Leisure*, we believe that travel changes everything—it changes you, and the exposure, wisdom, and openness you gain can even help change the world.

Andrea and Tony Malmberg, owners of the Twin Creek Ranch, in Lander, Wyoming.

UNITED
STATES
+CANADA

A SHORE BET

Classic Summers on Nantucket

THE TINY ISLAND OF NANTUCKET, with family compounds hidden behind privet hedges and a historic district with more than 800 pre–Civil War houses, has long been synonymous with the Old Guard. Downtown, Victorian bed-and-breakfasts share cobblestoned streets with tony boutiques and restaurants. With a few exceptions, the best stores lie in the heart of town, along Main, Federal, and Centre Streets. Murray's Toggery Shop is where you'll find the famous "Nantucket Red" trousers (which are actually pink), Sperry Top-Siders, and everything else locals

A boardwalk leading to the beachfront Wauwinet Inn.

Biking along the harbor in downtown Nantucket, above left. Above right: The Even Keel Café.

have been wearing since boarding school. Peter Beaton Hat Studio is the source for those lovely straw hats with the upturned brim and wide ribbon you see on all the women. The most delicious brunch is at Black-Eyed Susan's, a tiny café known for comfort food with a twist (French toast dipped in Jack Daniel's and topped with pecans). Come before 10 a.m. to avoid the crowd, or if the line is too long, head to the Even Keel Café, where the French toast comes battered in rum instead.

Unlike in other parts of Massachusetts, virtually all the beaches on Nantucket are open to the public. Great Point, steps away from the Wauwinet Inn in the northeast, has miles of secluded shoreline and sweeping views of the Atlantic. A white-shuttered, cedar-shingled classic, the 35-room Wauwinet was one of the first resorts built on Nantucket; it has as many

staff members as guests—not to mention bikes, kayaks, croquet and tennis courts, and sailboats—and the service is impeccable.

Several other great beaches, including Quidnet, are only a couple of miles outside of town. At Quidnet, there's no place to park, so the best way to get there is by bike. Rent a sporty Trek Hybrid (which comes with a traditional Nantucket wicker basket) at Young's Bicycle Shop, pick up one of their free maps of the island, and start exploring. +

For The Guide, see page 262.

The Institute of Contemporary Art, with the Boston skyline in the background.

ART IN RESIDENCE

Boston's Avant-Garde New Museum

ON A GRITTY WATERFRONT STRETCH OF South Boston, the Institute of Contemporary Art (ICA) has a bold new home, making it the first art museum to rise in Boston in nearly 100 years. Designed by the New York architectural firm Diller Scofidio + Renfro, the building—with its angular lines, dramatic glass-and-steel cantilever, and grandstand-cum-amphitheater—couldn't be more different from the institution's former space (a converted 19th-century police station).

Everything about the ICA goes against the traditional museum experience. Instead of ascending a grand staircase, you enter an unassuming glass door on the ground floor. Inside, one wall is devoted to commissioned artworks; the inaugural piece was an anime-style mural, *The Divine Gas*, by Japanese artist Chiho Aoshima. A glass-enclosed elevator brings visitors to two skylit top-floor galleries. Then there's Mediatheque, a hands-on "classroom" with computers, at which visitors can watch filmed interviews with artists whose works are being shown. The media center is stepped; at its far end a large window, at a 24-degree angle, frames a view of water so still, except for the occasional passing duck, that project architect Elizabeth Diller has called it the ultimate screen saver. ✦

For The Guide, see page 262.

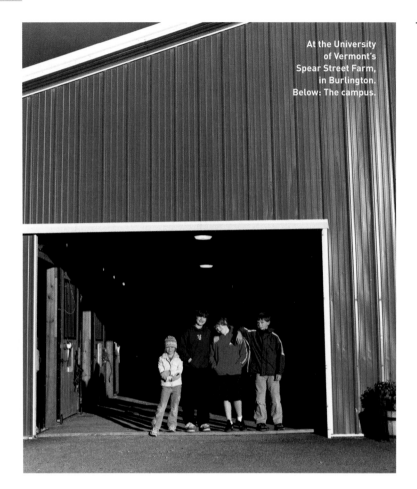

At the University of Vermont's Spear Street Farm, in Burlington. Below: The campus.

VERMONT OUTING

A Family Trip to Burlington

WITH A MATCHLESS LOCATION ON LAKE Champlain, between the Adirondack and Green Mountains, the college town of Burlington, Vermont, is remarkably family-friendly. Downtown is a pedestrian-only zone of smoothie parlors and found-art galleries. And just past the city limits, there are countless rivers to paddle, trails to hike, and hills to sled.

The University of Vermont, which sprawls across town, is a surprising place for young children to learn about science. At the Perkins Geology Museum, the fossil collection includes an ancient whale skeleton found in sediment nearby and a free-for-the-taking pile of discarded specimens. On the south end of campus, the Paul Miller Research Complex (a.k.a. Spear Street Farm) is where agriculture students learn to manage cows, sheep, and pigs. Visitors are welcome to watch the daily milking from 2 p.m. to 4 p.m. Walk among the apple trees and pick up snacks at the college's 97-acre Horticultural Research Center, known as Hort Farm.

Or you can be sedentary: the Flynn Center for the Performing Arts, in a restored vaudeville house, has a schedule of Broadway shows and children's theater. This is one field trip the kids will never forget. ✢

For The Guide, see page 262.

The living room of Philip Johnson's 1949 Glass House, on the architect's former estate in New Canaan.

SHEER BEAUTY

Philip Johnson's Connecticut Masterpiece

ONE OF THE MOST CELEBRATED PRIVATE RESIDENCES of the 20th century, the Glass House—built by the late architect Philip Johnson in New Canaan—was opened to the public in 2007. Johnson, who helped bring the spare International Style of the Bauhaus movement to the United States, bequeathed the house and its accompanying 14 buildings to the National Trust for Historic Preservation in 1986, with the idea that it would function as a museum after his death. Only 60 people per day are permitted on the 47-acre estate, open from April through October. The landscaping is so carefully planned that there is no possibility of on-site parking, so guests are brought to the site by a van from a small visitors' center near the New Canaan train station.

To visit the diverse constellation of structures is to accompany Johnson on a tour of his own history of architectural styles. Inspired by Ludwig Mies van der Rohe, the house, completed in 1949, consists of a single room with floor-to-ceiling transparent walls held together by a steel frame. And outside, the property is sprinkled with design follies, like a lakeside staircase leading to nowhere but the sky. **✦**

For The Guide, see page 262.

BITES OF THE BIG APPLE

Where In-the-Know New Yorkers Are Eating Now

The Spotted Pig, on a West Village corner, left.
Below: A pie at Una Pizza Napoletana.
Opposite: Chef David Chang tasting oysters at
Momofuku Noodle Bar.

FOR CULINARY THRILL-SEEKERS and casual chowhounds alike, there's never been a better moment to dine in Manhattan. The Great Restaurant Boom that began a few years ago shows no sign of abating. For every celebrity-driven showcase, there's a cultish small dining bar presided over by a young culinary alchemist or green-market guru.

Worth the splurge is L'Atelier de Joël Robuchon, the Manhattan branch of the French chef's ever-expanding galaxy of haute restaurants. Bury your spoon into a silken cauliflower purée to unearth bits of lobster and nuggets of sea urchin. You'll taste pristine tuna sashimi and tender house-cured pastrami. End with the "sucre" dessert: milk foam and violet custard in a sugar balloon bejeweled with raspberry gelée; it's the closest you'll come to sinking your teeth into a Fabergé egg.

At Per Se, prepare for a lesson in salt, illustrated with silver bowls of rare Hawaiian varieties to spike up your foie gras.

You'll also be treated to squab, eggs, and butter from boutique farmers; house-made chocolates in flavors like orange blossom; and a wine list rich in reasonably priced German finds.

Despite the multitude of brand-name chefs and trillion-dollar interiors, Korean-American David Chang's narrow Momofuku Noodle Bar, in the East Village, has become Manhattan's zeitgeist restaurant, sparking a craze for bar dining. It's worth the wait for feathery Chinese buns filled with rich slabs of Berkshire pork and kimchi-zapped

A sampling of Doughnut Plant's 70 varieties, below. Right: L'Atelier de Joël Robuchon. Opposite: Clinton St. Baking Co. & Restaurant, on the Lower East Side.

oysters. The counter culture continues at Degustation's 16-seat bar, which turns out tapas-scaled triumphs such as foie gras in caramel water.

A quintessential neighborhood restaurant, the West Village's Spotted Pig is a hip gastropub that won a Michelin star for its earthy British-Italian cooking. Lunch is bliss, from the warmth of the porcine-themed tavern to the high-octane smoked haddock chowder, and *gnudi* that taste like ricotta dumplings from heaven. Order a pint of frothy-smooth Old

Speckled Hen and discreetly study your neighbors' tattoos.

In New York, Italian is still innovative. Squeezed into a Clinton Street storefront, Falai is a Euro-chic trattoria that harbors such adventurous notions as octopus with candied-celery garnish and potato-sausage ravioli chased by apple consommé. The place is the vision of Iacopo Falai, once a pastry chef at Le Cirque. To try the apotheosis of a standard slice, visit Una Pizza Napoletana, where four types of pies prove that less is indeed *molto*.

For proof that food stars don't shine only at night, sample one of the 70 kinds of yeast-raised beauties with glazes like apricot and grapefruit at Doughnut Plant, in Chinatown. Or, head to Clinton St. Baking Co. & Restaurant on the Lower East Side, where dedicated locals drag themselves out of bed for fluffy buttermilk biscuits and blueberry pancakes. +

For The Guide, see page 262.

HARLEM IS HAUTE

Gotham Style Hunters Head Uptown

MANHATTAN'S NORTHERN REACHES HAVE become the city's latest fashionable destination, with a clutch of boutiques opening up around a historic stretch of 125th Street.

Designer Montgomery Harris was among the first to colonize the area. Her pioneering store carries short, ruched-sleeve jackets in men's wear fabrics and illustrated T-shirts—many of which she creates herself.

It's no surprise that Atmos, the hugely popular Tokyo sneaker store, selected Harlem as the site for its first stateside outpost. The company collaborates with athletic giants like Nike and Reebok to create custom shoes. Japanese fashion is also afoot at Denim Library—another source for obscure labels. The shop carries 35 brands, including Japan's high-end lines Ciano Farmer and Red Monkey.

But the biggest news around 125th Street is the 4,000-square-foot N, the neighborhood's largest designer boutique. Think Hugo Boss for men, and Nicole Miller and Iman Cosmetics for women—just a few reasons why the shop is often referred to as the Barneys of Harlem. ✦

For The Guide, see page 263.

Montgomery Harris (*seated*) and a client in her shop, Montgomery, in Harlem.

Outdoor dining at Café Saint-Ex, in the U Street Corridor, right. Below: At Project 4 gallery, on U Street.

CAPITAL COMEBACK

Transforming a D.C. Neighborhood

AS WASHINGTON, D.C.'S INNER CITY BLOSSOMS, the roughly six contiguous areas known as MidCity are hosting an influx of artists and professionals. At its heart, Logan Circle (a Victorian residential quarter in its day) and the U Street Corridor (once hailed as Black Broadway, where hometown hero Duke Ellington grew up) were among the city's most embattled neighborhoods. Now businesses are opening in a collaborative spirit.

At galleries like Project 4, guest curators organize shows (photography, sculpture) by D.C. artists. Boutiques carry furniture from Asia, fashion from Europe, and "vegan-friendly" vinyl bags.

At night, DJ's spin at Gate 54, a moody lounge with a speakeasy vibe; on iPod evenings, locals plug in their own collections. Named for a 1987 House resolution honoring jazz, the nonprofit HR-57 is dedicated to preserving the groove in an area once thick with clubs featuring performers such as Miles Davis and Sarah Vaughan. The Duke would be proud. +

For The Guide, see page 263.

A display of mirrors at Table 1280, in downtown Atlanta.

TABLE HOPPING

Atlanta's Top Restaurants

FROM THE EMERGING DISTRICT OF ATLANTIC Station to preppy Inman Park, Atlanta's restaurants are showcasing Georgia's homegrown culinary talents.

At Lobby at Twelve, in Atlantic Station, chef Nick Oltarsh's confident New American cooking is on display in dishes like Georgia trout with

The Woodruff Arts Center's main piazza in downtown Atlanta, above. Left: Chef Clifford Harrison holding cured meats and bread at Quinones.

lemon-tomato fondue.

In the $124 million Renzo Piano extension to the Woodruff Arts Center, in downtown Atlanta, Table 1280 is a study in elegant minimalism; two soaring, light-drenched white rooms offer little in the way of embellishment beyond a pair of art installations. The setting alone is worth the price of a meal, which says a lot. The ambitious dinner menu includes soulful short ribs enlivened by horseradish and salsa verde, and white-chocolate cake with hints of fennel.

Krogbar is a pocket-size, amber-lit wine bar with an upscale, log-cabin feel, where Inman Park loft dwellers share plates of bresaola and lemony roasted artichokes under patio heaters.

At Quinones, Clifford Harrison and Anne Quatrano preach the Alice Waters gospel and dream up sophisticated—but not fussy—10-course tasting menus composed of heirloom produce from their farm. Every single dish on the Westside restaurant's prix fixe menu, including the Virginia wild striped bass with slivers of Meyer lemon, proves that New Southern cooking doesn't get any tastier than this. ✛

For The Guide, see page 263.

Erwin Wurm's *UFO*, in Collins Park, left. Below: *Shelter (Charis)*, an installation from Austria-based Galerie Grita Insam.

BASEL DAZZLE

The Splashy Miami Beach Art Fair

MIAMI THRIVES ON THE FUN-ABOVE-ALL PRINCIPLE of nightclubs, and the idea that the Swiss fair Art Basel would pick the city as its sole satellite has a certain loopy logic. Despite the fair's focus on edgy contemporary art, Basel itself was (and remains) the polite embodiment of old-line Europe; Miami, which hosts Art Basel Miami Beach every December, is all about the shock of the New World, still raw and resolutely democratic—a tropical frontier that's the ideal blank canvas.

Beyond the fair itself at the Miami Beach Convention Center, with galleries from 30 countries, the festivities are spreading ever wider each year. On South Beach, there is Art Positions, where cutting-edge galleries set up camp in freight containers. There are also a head-spinning number of alternative fairs taking over hotels along Collins Avenue. To the north, the upscale Design District hosts Design Miami, an event with installations by luminaries on the order of Yoko Ono.

And then there are the parties. The nocturnal landscape is crowded with fashion shows, neo-burlesque revues, and performance art. ✦

For The Guide, see page 263.

Poolside at the Hotel San José. Left: Jo's Coffee Shop.

HEART OF TEXAS

Tuning In to Austin's Vibe

LIFE IN THIS LAID-BACK TOWN HAS COME a long way from sipping Shiner Bock at a backyard barbecue. High-tech whiz kids and Hollywood heavyweights have migrated to Austin—though it still holds on to its distinctly Texan identity. This is the land of unhurried and unpretentious cool, a reincarnated hippiedom in which art and music of all sorts are celebrated.

The best place to experience the city's energy is along South Congress Avenue, between Oltorf Street to the south and the Town Lake to the north, a quirky neighborhood that has been dubbed SoCo.

At Jo's Coffee Shop, pick up an iced turbo coffee. Nearby, Uncommon Objects overflows with vintage clothing, antique medical instruments, and other oddities. By George is the source for dresses by Lewis Cho and J Brand jeans.

If you go to Austin and don't stop at the legendary Continental Club, you haven't really seen the city; it's Austin's top spot for live music. Be sure to book a room at SoCo's Hotel San José. Born a Spanish Colonial motor court in the mid-1930's, the hotel today practices a monastic edginess, with concrete floors and spare appointments. Every Thursday night, guests are joined by Austinites, flocking to its parking lot, folding chairs in hand, to see area bands. ✚

For The Guide, see page 263.

STRIKING STRUCTURES

An Architecture Drive Through the Midwest

CALL IT THE BILBAO EFFECT. THESE DAYS, some of the country's most exciting architecture can be found in the Midwest. The best way to see it: on a road trip through Ohio, Indiana, Wisconsin, Minnesota, and Iowa.

Start at the complex of electrifying Morphosis-designed buildings at the University of Cincinnati. It's topped by a massive dorm—a V-shaped, cantilevered superblock with a chunk missing in the middle. Then head downtown, to Zaha Hadid's Contemporary Arts

Santiago Calatrava's new addition to the Milwaukee Art Museum, in Wisconsin.

The Toledo Museum of Art's Glass Pavilion, above. Opposite, clockwise from top left: Stephen Holl's School of Art and Art History, at the University of Iowa; the hand-crafted concrete supports of the Baumgartner Galleria, in the Milwaukee Art Museum's Quadracci Pavilion; the second-floor library of the School of Art and Art History; a dashboard view of Indiana's cornfields, on I-90.

Center. The jutting concrete-and-glass structure is bursting with energy; the columns are trapezoids, the doors parallelograms.

It's a straight shot from Cincinnati to Toledo, where the Toledo Museum of Art's Glass Pavilion—designed by SANAA, a critically admired Japanese firm—seems like a basic glass box, but is deceptively sophisticated. You can stand in a gallery and look through glass walls to watch artists at work, and, beyond, the park outside, all in one uninterrupted view.

When the gleaming Santiago Calatrava addition to the Milwaukee Art Museum opened in 2001, art lovers descended on the Rust Belt. Framed by Lake Michigan, Calatrava's Pavilion is a poetic form that evokes the shapes of ships (of both sea and space).

On to Minneapolis, where the Herzog & de Meuron extension of the Walker Art Center deflects light in unusual ways, making what is essentially a box seem dynamic in shape.

Central Iowa is so featureless, you can spot Des Moines from 10 miles away. There, David Chipperfield's quietly radical Des Moines Public Library is a low-slung building clad in a perforated-copper skin. You'll find Stephen Holl's School of Art and Art History 114 miles away, in Iowa City, on the campus of the University of Iowa. It's a buoyant hulk sheathed in weathered steel panels. The showstopper is the central staircase, a soaring collage of steel and cables. A third-floor walk-up has never been so appealing. +

For The Guide, see page 264.

Chef Shawn McClain of Custom House, left. Below: Foie gras brulée with macadamia nuts at Custom House. Opposite: Trattoria-inspired Quartino.

CHICAGO HEATS UP

The White-Hot Culinary Scene in the Second City

MASTERS LIKE CHARLIE TROTTER and Rick Bayless long ago helped Chicago shed its "Hog Butcher for the World" image. Now the city is peppered with young chefs who are blending straight-from-the-farm food with inventive technique.

Grant Achatz has been igniting the most sparks with his kitchen-as-laboratory approach at Alinea, where he atomizes, spindles, and otherwise manipulates food into flavor-packed combinations of powders, foams, and globules. The waitstaff decipher Achatz's complex menu like seasoned chemists. Diners can choose a 12-course tasting menu or a 24-course grand tour—and should plan on staying for at least three hours.

Known for working his magic with fish (at Spring) and vegetables (at Green Zebra), Shawn McClain is now sinking his teeth into red meat at Custom House. Steaks are the stars; try the crusty pan-roasted prime sirloin.

With walls covered in subway tiles and shelves groaning with freshly baked artisanal breads, Quartino is a charming, old-world Italian spot for small plates. Witness the duck prosciutto, which is cured on-site.

It's easy to drive right past Schwa, tucked behind a dingy storefront in Wicker Park. Don't. Beyond the squeaky front door lies a tiny BYOB spot, where the laid-back vibe and ambitious food will win you over. +

For The Guide, see page 264.

ROCKY MOUNTAIN HIGH

Serene Skiing in the Colorado Town of Breckenridge

WHEN IT COMES TO COLORADO RESORT TOWNS, athletes, adventurers, celebrities, and tycoons have long gravitated toward Aspen and Vail. But in recent years, Breckenridge has started to gain traction. The reasons: less attitude than its posh neighbors and price tags as soft as its powder.

At the Four Peaks Inn, a cheerful red Victorian house set in the heart of the ski village, book the Mountain Vista room, an aerie on the top floor. From beneath the down on the four-poster bed, you can peer out at the Colorado Rockies.

After an English-style breakfast of sausage, eggs, bacon, and sautéed mushrooms, laid out in the inn's sunlit dining area, stroll over to Main Street, where turn-of-the-20th-century houses from Breckenridge's mining days have been transformed

T+L Tip

Wake up late? Take advantage
of the discounted 12-p.m.-to-
4-p.m. half-day lift pass.

Boot rentals at Colorado Free Ride, above left. Above right: The Mountain Vista room at the Four Peaks Inn. Opposite: A view of the mountains from the Vista Haus chalet.

into brightly painted boutiques. Stock up on all the necessary gear at Colorado Free Ride, a two-story, one-stop shop for skiers on the north end of town, before heading to Peak 9, one of the mountain's four base areas.

Breckenridge is mostly known for its moderate, gentle runs, but the challenging slopes around the new Imperial Bowl at the peak are changing that reputation. The Imperial Express chairlift, which takes you to 12,840 feet up, is the highest in North America—and the views from the top alone are worth the trip, even if the hill below looks a bit precipitous. Between runs, warm up at the mountainside Vista Haus with a cup of hot chocolate. The blond-wood chalet has a mod-Scandinavian feel and a terrace overlooking the fir-lined valley.

After dark, Breckenridge turns into a storybook winter village: fresh snow on the sidewalk, lights-strewn trees, and bracingly crisp night air. Below the pressed-tin ceiling of the South Ridge Seafood Grill, you'll find real-estate magnates and scruffy snowboarders sitting side by side at a long, marble-topped bar. Whether dressed in a sports blazer or a ski jacket, everyone bears the same mark of the mountain: a goggle tan. +

For The Guide, see page 264.

TRUE WEST

Wyoming's Cowboy Country

THE WORD *COWBOY* HAS BECOME so associated with coolness, sexiness, and the Marlboro Man, the fact that it is made up of "cow" as much as "boy" seems to have been all but lost. While the meaning of the word in our collective unconscious has changed, you can still find the original cowboys' landscape preserved in certain parts of northern Wyoming.

In Sheridan, at the many-gabled Sheridan Inn, where Buffalo Bill Cody auditioned acts for his Wild West shows, you can eat steaks in the shade of the trophied heads of some rather large stuffed beasts—elk and moose, mountain goats and mountain lions. Farther south, in Buffalo, is the Occidental Hotel, the oldest in the state, whose saloon hosted, on various occasions, Calamity Jane and Rough Rider Teddy Roosevelt.

In the foothills of the Owl Creek Mountains, the town of Thermopolis is an oddity, given that it appears to be waiting for tourists in a way that no other part of northern Wyoming is. Thermopolis is the site of the world's largest mineral hot springs, which feeds the modest, Modernist facilities of the State Bath House. You can get in free for 20 minutes, just by signing the

The hills outside the
Wyoming town of Thermopolis,
on the Big Horn River.

Travis James "T.J." Clark, a rodeo cowboy.

The Irma Hotel, in Cody.

WATERING HOLES

These are the top spots in Wyoming to pull up a stool and have a drink—most likely, next to a cowboy.

Cowboy Bar Butch Cassidy was arrested here in 1894 for stealing a horse.

Elk Horn Bar & Grill The ceiling above the pool tables is covered with hundreds of cowboy boots of all shapes, sizes, and designs.

Buffalo Bill's Irma Hotel Restaurant & Saloon A hotel built by Buffalo Bill himself in 1902. The old-time saloon is a good spot to cool off.

Proud Cut Saloon & Restaurant Cold beers and, as the menu says, kick-ass cowboy cuisine.

register. Or, check out the Star Plunge, an indoor-outdoor water park with a 500-foot-long slide. After a buffalo burger at Pumpernicks, a family-run café on the main street, inspect the dozens of sandstone petroglyphs at Legend Rock, a historic site near the town of Hamilton Dome.

The night rodeo in Cody isn't like the ones you see on television. Young riders from as far away as Australia and Brazil come here to train, staying in their saddles only a blurred, scary second or two. The horses and bulls—charging and snorting—get at least as much admiration as the riders.

It's at the Old Trail Town, on the outskirts of Cody, however, that you'll see how the old-time wranglers lived. Twenty-five buildings, dating from 1879 to 1901, have been moved here. There are original buffalo-hunter, carpenter, and blacksmith cabins; a saloon; and a post office. You can even tour the two-room cabin where Butch Cassidy and the Sundance Kid and other members of the infamous "Hole in the Wall" gang gathered to plan their next heist—it's a flashback to America's West. +

For The Guide, see page 264.

Climbing the Gap, near the Red Mountain Spa, in Ivins, Utah. Below: Spa guests in typical afternoon attire.

DESERT OASIS

Outdoor Adventures at a Utah Spa

EVEN IF YOU'RE NOT A SPA PERSON, WHEN you arrive at Red Mountain, you may forget both your skepticism and your goals. There's no deprivation (butter, beer, and wine are on offer), but more significantly, there's no lack of visual stimulation. The display of sandstone domes, red-rock spires, dunes, volcanic deposits, and eccentrically weathered stone columns make the area a living geology lesson. And if the Pueblo Indians had built condominiums, the structures might have looked like the buildings here, with names like Quail, Owl, and Armadillo.

Devotees are attracted to Red Mountain's reputation as an adventure spa, which means there is an emphasis on rugged and sometimes risky outdoor activities. You can rock climb or kayak near Zion National Park, spend a day exploring Bryce Canyon, or take a two-day, 26-mile hike through the Grand Canyon. There's also the promise of transformation, of coming back thinner, healthier, and stronger, thanks to conventional classes like tai chi, circuit training, and Aqua Asana (essentially yoga in the pool). And let's not forget, you're permitted, even encouraged, to wear a robe and slippers on the premises at all times. +

For The Guide, see page 265.

LAS VEGAS NIGHTS

Doing Sin City for Less

Mix Lounge at the Hotel at Mandalay Bay, in Las Vegas.

LAS VEGAS HAS ALWAYS CATERED to high rollers. Each new casino is more luxe than the last. But play your cards right and you can spend a fun night in Sin City even if you don't bet like a billionaire.

To avoid the cover charge at Mix Lounge, on the 64th floor of the Hotel at Mandalay Bay, arrive before 10 p.m. It has glowing round tables and floor-to-ceiling windows with 360-degree views of the Strip, making for the best show in town. Decamp for dinner to the Buffet at TI, part of a new breed of $20 smorgasbords. The Jeffrey Beers–designed dining room is sleek, and the seven flavors of home-made ice cream alone make it worth the trip. Next, hit the nearby Venetian Casino for a free blackjack lesson before heading to Pure, the club in Caesars Palace. Get your name on the list by calling ahead, and you'll breeze right past the throngs. ✛

For The Guide, see page 265.

A DAY AT THE PARK

The Best of Disneyland

LIKE A FRANK O'HARA POEM or a Norman Rockwell painting, Disneyland is both completely of its time and ageless. Since its opening in 1955, the park has been famous for intricate foot-traffic control and for its self-contained feeling (at almost no point can you see anything of the world outside).

Disneyland is the single-minded creation of Walt Disney, a cheerfully eccentric man who translated his scrawlings into millions of tons of concrete and steel. The guy liked railroads: you can still see his private car, the *Victorian Lilly Belle*, tacked to the rear of the choo-choo that circles the park. His nifty trip to the real French Quarter resulted in the beautifully detailed New Orleans Square, with wrought-iron balconies, Mardi Gras beads, and an army of Preservation Hall–grade Dixieland bands.

Arrive by 8 a.m., and you'll whip through more rides before 10 a.m. than you will in the next eight hours. Start with Soarin'

A marching band at Disneyland, in Anaheim, California.

The Dumbo ride, flying since 1955, above left. Above right: Fireworks over Sleeping Beauty's castle.

T+L Tip

There are countless ticket options, but plan to spend $60 to $80 per day per person for entrance, parking, and snacks. To fully experience the park, it takes about three days, so if there's a slight chance you may return to the area within a year, opt for the cheapest annual pass available ($229 per person).

Over California, a simulated hang-glider trip around the state and possibly the best Disney ride ever. Next, go right to Indiana Jones Adventure, where Humvee-like vehicles take you through swarming spiders, abrupt drops, and a profusion of Audio-Animatronic Harrison Fords. And be sure to chart a course for Space Mountain, a medium-size steel coaster shrouded in darkness.

Finally, don't miss the top two spectacles. Fantasmic! is a presentation involving lasers, pirate ships, and rivers exploding into flame. And then there are the fireworks. As she has every night for decades, Tinkerbell swoops to Sleeping Beauty's castle at about 9:15 p.m. for a pyrotechnics show that lights up the kingdom. +

For The Guide, see page 265.

CITY OF FASHION

The Shopping Mecca of Melrose Heights

Inside the Paul Smith boutique on Melrose Avenue in Los Angeles.

MELROSE HEIGHTS, A LOS ANGELES shopping destination since the eighties, has turned high-end thanks to a clutch of designer shops that have opened in the area. For an ideal walking tour, start at Paul Smith's

5,000-square-foot loftlike space on the corner of Melrose and Harper Avenues. Inside, you'll find a comprehensive collection of pieces that display the British designer's cheeky aesthetic, including Union Jack–upholstered chairs.

Continue west along Melrose to Suzanne Felsen. The glowing Modernist façade is a perfect complement to the shop's gemstone jewelry. Next up is Duncan Quinn. This men's wear atelier brings Savile Row tailoring and a rock 'n' roll edge to West Hollywood.

The neighborhood's beacon of style, Marc Jacobs, sits on Melrose Place and Melrose Avenue. Across the street is Marc by Marc Jacobs, his less pricey label, with its playful, L.A.-friendly looks. Mirrored ceilings at Diane von Furstenberg's store create a glam backdrop for her updated wrap dresses and fine-jewelry collection for H.Stern.

Delia, an emporium of lesser-known European designers, is hidden above a breezy courtyard a few doors down. Pair your discoveries with vintage sunglasses from nearby RetroSpecs.

End the trip with a stop at Temperley London, where fans slip in for cowl-necked dresses that have been seen on Uma Thurman and Sienna Miller, both of whom you might run into while browsing. After all, this is Hollywood. ✦

For The Guide, see page 265.

At Temperley London, above. Right: A display at Paul Smith. Opposite: Striking a pose at Marc by Marc Jacobs.

UP AT THE GETTY VILLA

Classical Antiquities in Malibu

WITH THE CREATION OF THE RICHARD MEIER–DESIGNED, billion-dollar Getty Center in Los Angeles in 1997, the much-loved Roman-style villa the museum once called home began to fade from the city's cultural memory. This was hardly surprising: the old museum, in a loose re-creation of a first-century villa on oil-tycoon J. Paul Getty's Malibu ranch, was hidden in a canyon off the Pacific Coast Highway. But with the reopening of the renovated Getty Villa, housing preeminent collections of Roman, Greek, and Etruscan antiquities, classical architecture is again front and center. In the modern buildings, a rich variety of materials allude to the palette of Roman structures: black marble from China, teak-like wood. And once-dark galleries are bathed in light—preferable for viewing classical statuary. The ancient world has never looked better. +

For The Guide, see page 265.

The Entry Pavilion at the Getty Villa, designed by Machado & Silvetti.

A vineyard on the road to Healdsburg, in California's Sonoma County, left. Below: Barndiva's general manager, Lukka Feldman, behind the bar.

THE NEW WINE COUNTRY

Sonoma's Latest Destination

"EAT LOCAL" IS A RALLYING CRY throughout northern California, but in Healdsburg, an hour's drive from San Francisco, many chefs are putting their menus where their mouths are. The town began its transformation in 2001, with the arrival of the Hotel Healdsburg, co-owned by Charlie Palmer. The hotel is also home to the restaurant Dry Creek Kitchen, where the chef spotlights regional purveyors. The most notable newcomer is rising chef Douglas Keane's Cyrus: the maître d' phones Keane to announce your arrival, cuing the tableside champagne-and-caviar cart.

The liveliest scene in town is found at Barndiva, a big red barn with late-night meals and creative cocktails. This being wine country, there are more than 12 tasting rooms located within a mile of Healdsburg's main plaza. The best: Thumbprint Cellars, for its small-lot wines, and Toad Hollow, for its no-oak Chardonnay.

While neighboring Napa was always thought to be more civilized, Les Mars Hotel shows just how far Sonoma has come. Modeled after a French château, the 16 rooms are decked out with four-poster canopy beds, and 17th- and 18th-century antiques. +

For The Guide, see page 265.

LAVA LAND

A Tour of Hawaii Volcanoes National Park

Swimmers at the volcanically heated Ahalanui pond, in Kilauea, on the southeastern edge of Hawaii, above. Right: Signs pointing the way in Kilauea. Opposite: A trek across cooled lava fields in Hawaii Volcanoes National Park.

DRAWN TO THE PROSPECT OF SEEING LAND BEING BORN, 2.5 million people a year visit Hawaii's Kilauea, the world's most active volcano. Located in the 333,000-acre Hawaii Volcanoes National Park, on the southeastern edge of the Big Island, the ruggedly beautiful Kilauea is often called "the drive-in volcano," because paved roads allow you to traverse it by car. The 11-mile paved road that circles the roughly six-square-mile caldera, or crater, is a mostly barren expanse of rock dotted with steam vents. It's big and blackish-brown and mottled, like an enormous pan of burned brownies. There's no molten lava in sight here—it lurks 300 feet below the surface.

An 11-mile hike toward Puu Oo, Kilauea's currently erupting vent, involves climbing through jagged rock and lush tree-fern forests to the rim, where the vent's broken cinder belches white, billowy smoke. A half-hour south of the road between the park and Hilo is Ahalanui, a "hot pond"; the pool is set in lava rock and fed by both the ocean and a freshwater spring that is volcanically heated to between 91 and 95 degrees. Spend a few relaxing hours basking and floating in the palm-fringed idyll. And be sure to pull over at Halemaumau, a quarry-like and sulfur-stained 300-foot-deep crater-within-the-crater where Pele, the Hawaiian goddess of fire, is said to live.

Thrill-seekers will want to drive 45

Inside a lava tube at Kilauea, above. Left: An aerial view of Kilauea's lava flowing into the Pacific.

T+L Tip

Enlist Tropical Helicopters to take you on an airborne tour of the most dramatic spots.

minutes down Chain of Craters Road, the park's winding path to the ocean, at dusk to witness the interaction of molten rock and sea. Park your car by the water—the view while coming down from the hill is of miles and miles of hardened and flowing lava that have been spilling into the sea since 1983—and then walk about 30 minutes to a spot on the beach. Two miles off in the distance, huge plumes of smoke form where the lava drips into the water, oozing into the ocean, puddling on the shore, and frantically streaming underneath the vent. The scene is mesmerizing, and as the lava grows darker, its glow becomes more pronounced and it lights up in a manner that's almost Oz-like. Here, where Kilauea has created more than 700 acres of new land in the past 26 years, you may find yourself walking on ground younger than you are. +

For The Guide, see page 266.

SCENIC BYWAYS

Drive Along Northeast Canada's Coastal Roads

TINY LUNENBURG, AN 18TH-CENTURY fishing village that's just an hour's drive south of the Halifax airport, is the perfect starting point for a weeklong drive between Nova Scotia and Prince Edward Island, in search of crafts, coastline, and authentic local oddities.

The village's downtown is a UNESCO World Heritage Site, and the surrounding area slopes to a bay lined on the far side by rolling swaths of green lawn. Lunenburg itself feels sleepy but

The Cabot Trail
on the tip of
Cape Breton Island,
in Nova Scotia.

The Inn at Bay
Fortune, on Prince
Edward Island, left.
Below: The Rusty
Anchor restaurant,
in Cape Breton's
Pleasant Bay.

arty—a place where locals dreamily strum acoustic guitars on their porches. At the end of the day, visit Lunenburg's charming, minimalist Fleur de Sel for bouillabaisse and panko-crusted frogs' legs.

It's a six-hour-drive north to verdant Prince Edward Island. The Inn at Bay Fortune, a handsome, shingled compound, once belonged to Colleen Dewhurst, who played the foster mother in *Anne of Green Gables*, which was set on the island. Dinner features just-caught seafood, vegetables raised from heirloom seeds, and the inn's garden salad, composed of 30 different greens grown on site. A screened-in porch overlooks a huge lawn and the bay, and nearby, potato fields seem to stretch for miles.

Another six-hour drive brought us to Cape Breton Island, where we picked up the Cabot Trail, a spectacular 180-mile road tracing the island's northern tip, decked out with sweeping turns, jagged cliffs, and a riot of antiques shops. Co-op Artisanale, in Chéticamp, has heaps of handmade rugs and socks; Leather Works, in Indian Brook, stocks handsome leather buckets; and Myles from Nowhere, a funky, two-story shack on the side of the road in Margaree Forks, is all about campy

glamour. Halfway down the road, be sure to stop at the Rusty Anchor, in Pleasant Bay, where the lobster-themed menu is announced by a large statue of a fisherman along the road.

Cape Breton is also where you'll find the small Elizabeth LeFort Museum, dedicated to one of the world's foremost rug hookers. LeFort's hooked-wool portraits of Jackie Kennedy and various Canadian prime ministers are astonishing in their obsessiveness, as is her depiction of the Resurrection, which measures 80 square feet and required eight miles of yarn and 2 million stitches. +

For The Guide, see page 266.

COLD COMFORT

Quebec City's Winter Charms

THERE'S AN INTIMACY TO QUEBEC CITY in winter. The walls that contain it, and the bitter chill, tend to draw people together. Quebec City teaches you how to embrace the season's rawness—not only to enjoy it, but to love it with conviction, as the surfer loves the leading edge of a hurricane.

Québécois food and drink is your wave in. Settled by French fur traders 400 years ago, the city has never lost its Gallic allure. There is a casual, distinctly quotidian quality to its food

Rue Buade in Vieux-Québec.

Vieux-Québec's Lower Town, a neighborhood of Quebec City, right. Below: A young hockey player at Place d'Youville's outdoor rink, in Upper Town.

life—excellent bread baked around every corner, shelves of local cheeses in neighborhood markets.

Despite its popularity as a tourist attraction, Quebec City's French character is genuine. At places like Café Le St.-Malo, which has a roaring fire in the hearth, you're not likely to find a single English-speaking patron.

From the bar at L'Astral, a restaurant on the 29th floor of a skyscraper just outside the city walls, you can see the St. Lawrence River across the rooftops, as well as the vertiginous cliffs that divide Vieux-Québec into an Upper and Lower Town, accentuating the angularity of the architecture, all gabled roofs and soaring turrets.

During Quebec City's Winter Carnival, which takes place every February, the streets of Upper Town fill with revelers. Head to the rink at Place d'Youville, where you can rent skates and take a turn in the crisp air.

A nightcap at the restored Auberge St.-Antoine is an ideal way to end the day. At the bar, request an aperitif called Neige, a *cidre de glace*: cider fermented from juice pressed out of apples frozen on the tree. Honeyed and viscous, with the aroma of Calvados, it is classic wintry Quebec: something warm squeezed from the ice. +

For The Guide, see page 266.

After hours at the Drake Hotel, in Toronto. Left: One of the hotel's 19 rooms.

TORONTO'S TIME
The Next Great Neighborhood

TORONTO IS LESS A CITY than an interconnecting set of intimate neighborhoods that has the feel of a string of independent villages. One of the more interesting areas is a bustling district that locals refer to as West Queen West (to distinguish it from a stuck-in-time section closer to downtown).

It was thanks to the Drake Hotel, a converted flophouse which arrived on the scene in 2004, that the neighborhood turned into a center for art, design, and music. In many ways, the Drake embodies the spirit percolating in Toronto. Almost as soon as it opened, the Drake became a magnet for bohemian types. Designed by the Toronto firm 3rd Uncle, the hotel's 19 rooms—which include "crash pads" and "dens"—are beyond eclectic: floral wallpaper, flea-market décor, and bathrooms set off by vinyl curtains or partly frosted glass doors.

Downstairs, the plywood dining room walls are covered in trippy felt Rorschach blots; the lounge has mismatched vintage chairs and leather sofas. There's also a raw bar, an exercise studio, a basement-level performance space, and the rooftop "sky yard," a covered outdoor deck.

After the sensory overload of the Drake, the spare, underdesigned Czehoski restaurant comes as a relief. The former butcher shop's faded sign still hangs above the front door. Its interiors are furnished with classic Mies

The Four Seasons Centre for the Performing Arts, above. Opposite, clockwise from top left: Camera, director Atom Egoyan's screening-room lounge; a local on Queen Street West; Czehoski chef Nathan Isberg; the Commute Home shop.

van der Rohe chairs and brown-velvet curtains. An old deli counter, once filled with selections of kielbasa, has been transformed into a wine fridge. And the cuisine is experimental, with items such as "butter-poached potatoes and five superfluous French beans."

Throughout, bars, galleries, and shops sit cheek by jowl. Camera, a screening-room lounge owned by filmmaker Atom Egoyan, is walking distance from boutiques like Delphic, which stocks Acne denim, and Commute Home, an industrial design store.

Nearby sits the Toronto Fashion Incubator, in a renovated warehouse building. There, private donors help subsidize 10 working studios for fashion designers. They even provide sewing machines. It is here that you'll find homegrown talent like Arthur Mendonça, the 32-year-old darling of the Canadian fashion scene, who has outfitted celebrities such as Maria Bello and Nelly Furtado.

The area's architecture is also gaining notice, with buildings by foreign architects and hometown designers. The Canadian Opera Company and National Ballet of Canada recently inaugurated their new venue: the Four Seasons Centre for the Performing Arts (named for their hotel company benefactor). By day, the simple, glass-enclosed box isn't as eye-popping as some of Toronto's other notable buildings (those by Alsop and Libeskind, for example), but at night it glows like a giant lantern. ✛

For The Guide, see page 266.

ART OF THE VINE

Canada's Okanagan Valley Wine Country

A selection from Carmelis Goat Cheese Artisan, in the town of Kelowna, left. Below: Richard Bullock, owner of Kelowna Orchard, in the valley. Opposite: Chardonnay and Pinot Noir grapes, at Mission Hill Family Estate, in Westbank, British Columbia.

BRITISH COLUMBIA'S OKANAGAN VALLEY runs for 125 miles along a chain of lakes that stretches from Armstrong, British Columbia, south to the Washington border. The views are spectacular: imagine Lake Tahoe as a backdrop for Napa Valley. Pinot Noirs and Rieslings are the headliners, but producers offer everything from robust reds to ice wines. There are only 5,300 acres of vines in the region, so little Okanagan wine leaves Canada. All the more reason to come taste it in person.

Base yourself in Kelowna. Ignore the motel-like sign and book a room at Hotel Eldorado, a lakeside lodge with claw-foot bathtubs, fireplaces, and cork floors. Pick up a sweet, nutty Parmesan or raw-milk chèvre from Carmelis Goat Cheese Artisan for an afternoon picnic in the vines.

Start your winery hopping at CedarCreek, which comes alive each summer with sunset concerts. The winery's ripe, high-acid Ehrenfelser is made from a Riesling-Sylvaner cross and crafted by ponytailed Californian Tom DiBello. The on-site restaurant serves game sausages and other wine-friendly foods.

Nk'Mip Cellars, owned and operated by the Osoyoos Indian Band in a joint venture with national powerhouse Vincor Canada, is situated on a lake a mile from the Washington border. The 2005 Riesling, made from grapes from 25-year-old vines, is as

The terrace at Mission Hill Family Estate's restaurant, above. Opposite: Sunset over Okanagan Lake.

BEST BOTTLES

Wine shipped across the border may be delayed by customs—ask for Styrofoam shippers so bottles can be safely checked.

CedarCreek Estate's Select Chardonnay 2004 ($19) It isn't over-oaked, over-extracted, or over-anythinged.

Mission Hill Family Estate's S.L.C. Syrah (2004, $40) Now in its seventh vintage, this may be the valley's most polished red.

Nk'Mip Cellars's Qwam Qwmt Riesling Ice Wine 2005 ($53) Sweet but not unctuous, it's a worthy sibling to the renowned bottles of Jackson-Triggs and Inniskillin.

Quails' Gate Estate Winery's Chenin Blanc 2006 ($17.80) High-toned lemon flavors make this bottle a superior example of an under-appreciated grape.

gummy and minerally as a Riesling ought to be. There are also 44 new Santa Fe–style villas, outfitted with flat-screen TV's, along with a nine-hole golf course and the Desert & Heritage Centre.

Winemaker Grant Stanley grew up in Vancouver and New Zealand, and his whites at Quails' Gate Estate Winery split the difference between the tropical-fruit notes of a Kiwi bottling and the floral aromatics typical of the Okanagan region. The 2001 Reserve Pinot Noir is particularly delicious. The winery's glass-and-cedar Old Vines Patio Restaurant, which overlooks Okanagan Lake, serves imaginative seafood dishes, and a 10-room inn is in the works.

Mission Hill Family Estate, a modern take on old-world architecture, is one of the most impressive wineries anywhere; it sits on a rise above Okanagan Lake. Shakespeare is performed in an amphitheater, private dinners are served beneath a Chagall tapestry, and a gorgeous kitchen doubles as a cooking-class studio. Bottle for bottle, no Canadian property is more accomplished. The wines, such as the fragrant yet crisp Five Vineyards Pinot Blanc, can't match the splendor of their setting, but they come close. +

For The Guide, see page 266.

Off Seven Mile
Beach, on the
western shore of
Grand Cayman.

CARIBBEAN+
THE BAHAMAS

A view of Soufrière town, from St. Lucia's West Coast Road.

ON THE VERGE

St. Lucia Sets Its Sights on Luxury

ST. LUCIA IS A PLACE WHERE BIRDS-OF-PARADISE roam freely. Until the 1990's, banana production was the top industry. One of the Lesser Antilles' Windward Islands, it isn't as easily accessible as destinations like the Bahamas—which kept it off the radar for many years. That's about to change, as the island becomes the darling of the money-is-no-object traveler, thanks to an influx of hotels.

The new 57-suite Discovery at Marigot Bay is part of a $60 million project that also includes a 40-slip marina and village—all intended to position the once popular but now faded yachting hangout as an upscale port. Across the island, the competition is stiff at Cotton Bay Village, where a beachfront château comes complete with a dedicated man Friday. ("We didn't want to call them butlers," marketing director Michael Bryant says.) Perhaps the boldest play is being made by Jade Mountain, set atop the highest point of Anse Chastanet Resort. In the 24 suites, there is no "fourth wall" insinuating itself between the room and the view of the Pitons; each room is completely exposed to the elements. And that's not all. RockResorts is opening the $165 million Landings resort in December 2007. Next up is Cap Maison, a butler-staffed boutique hotel, scheduled for March 2008. Add to that a Ritz-Carlton (2009) and a Raffles (2010), and you have all the ingredients for an all-star Caribbean getaway. ✦

For The Guide, see page 267.

STACKING THE DECKS

The World's Biggest Cruise Ship

IF YOU CAN'T FATHOM THE SIZE of Royal Caribbean's *Freedom of the Seas*, the largest cruise ship on the planet, consider this: if it were stood on its bow, it would be taller than the Eiffel Tower. There are enough staterooms (1,815) to host 4,375 people—or all of the NFL, MLB, and NBA's players and coaches at once. At 160,000 tons, it weighs more than 32,000 adult elephants. In fact, the ship is so large that it sails only to Caribbean ports—Grand Cayman's George Town; Montego Bay, Jamaica—that can manage both its wide body and its sizable shore traffic.

Then there are the amenities: whirlpools cantilevered over the ocean; a barber shop; a boxing ring; and the H2O Zone, a Jeff Koons–meets–Toys "R" Us water park of tall, colorful sculptures that spout, spray, and cascade, inviting joyous squealing from kids who run around, under, and through them. But it's the FlowRider surf simulator that Royal Caribbean is betting will outdo any other ship on the seas. An enormous machine pushes 34,000 gallons of water a minute down a cushioned plastic slope to simulate a towering five-foot ocean wave. All told, the ship is living proof that bigger really is better. **+**

For The Guide, see page 267.

Looking toward the stern on *Freedom of the Seas*.

A studio at Concordia
Eco-Tents, on St. John's Maho Bay.

ECO CHIC

The High Life on St. John

WHEN IT COMES TO ECO-TRAVEL IN THE Caribbean, St. John has been a trail-blazer. Thanks to Laurance Rockefeller, whose land donation in 1956 turned two-thirds of the island into a national park, it is, and will remain, among the most pristine spots in the Caribbean.

Located within Virgin Islands National Park itself, Maho Bay Camps is hidden away in the surrounding tropical forest, with steep terrain that leads down to the bay. The solar- and wind-powered eco-compound's 114 tented, wooden-frame cabins are built on stilts and connected by two miles of raised wooden walkways designed to prevent soil erosion. Visitors fill drinking-water jugs at communal taps and leave solar pouches in the sun for hot showers at night.

Concordia Eco-Tents, the sister resort to Maho Bay, is equally friendly to the environment but has more creature comforts. On a palm-studded cliff above a beach known for some of the finest snorkeling in the region, Concordia's 35 space-age structures epitomize off-the-grid R&R. They have translucent, heat-repellent walls; built-in solar showers; rain-collecting cisterns; and private decks. At the hotel's new open-air terrace café, taking in the sunset, drink in hand, feels downright virtuous. ✛

For The Guide, see page 267.

VIRGIN ESCAPE

Where to Go in the British Virgin Islands

The bar at Deadman's Beach Bar & Grill on Peter Island, left. Below: Roast pork layered with snow pea salad at the Dove, in Tortola's Road Town. Opposite: The spa pool at Peter Island resort.

THE BRITISH VIRGIN ISLANDS—an archipelago of more than 50 sleepy isles—beg to be explored. But if you don't feel like renting a yacht, use one of the two main islands as a base.

Home to the main airport, Tortola used to be nothing more than a way station for travelers en route to other places in the BVI. Now it's a worthy destination in its own right. Scott Hart and Paloma Helm are doing their part to spiff up the scruffy capital, Road Town, with the Dove restaurant and wine bar. Housed in a 1908 gingerbread-trimmed cottage and filled with antiques, the restaurant serves dishes like spanakopita with a red-pepper *concassée*. Shops are popping up, too, including the well-edited housewares boutiques Hucksters and Cantik Interiors.

On the northern and western parts of the island, you'll find a quieter, gentler Tortola, one with roomy beaches and,

towering over it all, the 1,710-foot Mount Sage. Set among the ruins of a 17th-century sugar plantation on the nearly empty Apple Bay beach, the Sugar Mill Hotel is one of the BVI's best values. Down the road, the legendary Bomba's Shack is a crazy bar built from cast-off tin, license plates, and driftwood. On the east side of the island, Aragorn's Studio has grown from a gallery into a burgeoning arts center, where crafts-people teach basket weaving and coconut carving, and a shop carries handmade herbal soaps

The spa pool at Little Dix Bay, on Virgin Gorda, right. Below: The monthly Fireball Full Moon party at Aragorn's Studio, on Tortola.

and bags of locally harvested salt.

Don't miss a day trip to Peter Island, a 30-minute ferry ride from Tortola. The 1,800-acre private-island resort charges upwards of $900 a night for guests, but anyone can come by for the day and use the facilities, which include a sprawling spa with couples' suites, a top-notch restaurant, and white-sand beaches.

Across the channel, long and skinny Virgin Gorda is the location of choice for luxury resorts in the BVI. In the 1960's, Laurance Rockefeller put the island on the map with Little Dix Bay.

Rosewood Hotels recently revamped the resort with an Asia-meets-the-tropics style. In addition to spiffed-up rooms, there are lavish villas, a spa set around an infinity pool, and more activities (iguana hunts for the kids, nightly steel-drum bands) than most small towns. A few miles away at Bitter End Yacht Club, guests have access to a fleet of free whalers, Sunfish, and sailboards. On the other side of the bay is Biras Creek Resort, perfect for solitude seekers. Ride around its 140 acres on fat-tired bikes.

Beyond the hotels, there's Spanish Town (a who-cares-if-you-miss-it blip), the much-photographed Baths (a maze of grottoes beloved by snorkelers), and the dizzying drive up Virgin Gorda Peak. You won't find much in the way of diversions on Virgin Gorda—and that's the point. ✚

For The Guide, see page 267.

COLONIAL CARIBBEAN

Discovering the Spirit of Santo Domingo

YOU COULD EASILY SPEND A WEEK lazing on the silky beaches along the Dominican Republic's coast and never see its capital, Santo Domingo. But that would mean missing out on the New World's oldest city, built just after Christopher Columbus's arrival in 1492. More than five centuries of culture are still on display in the 12-block Colonial Zone. Anchoring this assemblage of gar-

The 16th-century
Palacio Consistorial,
in downtown
Santo Domingo.

risons, wide cobblestoned plazas, and pastel-painted alleyways is the Catedral Primada de América, the hemisphere's first church, built in 1521. It's surrounded by a shaded square lined with cafés and street vendors eager to shine your shoes, press a glass of fresh sugarcane juice for you, or sell you a hand-woven cane or coconut-palm-frond hat for a few pesos.

Just off the square is a pair of 16th-century fortresses: Fortaleza Santo Domingo and Fortaleza Ozama. The oldest military compounds in the Americas, they were built by Governor Nicolas de Ovando, whose former mansion now houses a Sofitel hotel. Ovando's public works projects also included the nearby Hospital de San Nicolas de Bari, which served the city's poor for more than four centuries and now lies in picturesque ruins.

Along El Conde, the pedestrian thoroughfare, you can pick up cigars and coffee of the finest quality. End the day with a meal at Mesón d'Bari, where the Spanish-Dominican menu (order the *cangrejo guisado*, fresh crab stewed in a piquant brown sauce) is a favorite of native son Oscar de la Renta. ✦

For The Guide, see page 267.

Catedral Primada de América at Santo Domingo's Parque Colón. Opposite, clockwise from top left: Mesón d'Bari restaurant on Calle Hostos; a vendor selling hats made of coconut-palm fronds; a corridor at Alcazar de Colón, a 16th-century palace; the beach at Tortuga Bay Hotel in Punta Cana.

GOLDEN SANDS

Living Large on Grand Cayman

Seven Mile Beach on Grand Cayman's west coast. Below: Local road signs. Opposite: Friday-night festivities at the Ritz-Carlton's Silver Palm Lounge.

THE CAYMAN ISLANDS are a golden sand-box. In addition to being home to most of the world's hedge funds, the main island of Grand Cayman is also a tax-free haven for global deal makers. There is no crime to speak of and a negative unemployment rate, which means that hedge-fund managers leave their doors unlocked and every native-born islander is guaranteed a job. The fact that more than half the residents are short-term employees only adds to the island's other-worldly shimmer.

The paradoxical everyday reality of the world's fifth-largest financial center is still something of a secret, at least to most of the 1 million passengers who disembark every year from the cruise ships in George Town Harbour and whose vision of the island is lim-ited to a few blocks of faded colonial buildings and duty-free jewelry stores. Yet the same qualities that have trans-formed an obscure isle into the Swit-zerland of the Caribbean also make Grand Cayman alluring for luxury hotels. Four Seasons and Mandarin Oriental are rumored to be acquir-ing properties here; Ritz-Carlton has already opened a beachfront resort, Jean-Michel Cousteau–branded nature tours, and a La Prairie spa.

Despite its world-class allure, Grand Cayman is still an island with all the pleasures and evils of any other small town. At lunchtime, Caymanians can be heard gossiping about their neigh-bors. "People drink, have affairs, and practice water sports," says local news anchorwoman Cindy Arie. "Especially on Sundays, when you can't work." ✛

For The Guide, see page 267.

BAHAMIAN STYLE

The Boutiques of Harbour Island

A shopkeeper at the Blue Rooster, on Harbour Island, above.
Right: The Sugar Mill Trading Company. Opposite: The Blue Rooster.

ARRIVE ON TINY HARBOUR ISLAND, in the Bahamas, and you'll see a colonial settlement as it might have appeared 50 years ago: Jordan almond–colored seaside cottages left over from Loyalist days, narrow streets that lead up rambling hills. The fashion crowd has also latched onto this 3½-mile-long spit of land, with its preternaturally pink beaches, and opened some of the best boutiques in the region.

Harbour Island has a unique uniform—expensive, but just a little bit careless—and these shops have mastered the look. Blue Rooster, a whitewashed space in an 1840 gingerbread Victorian cottage, is filled with shell-encrusted sandals and delicate pashmina shawls. Pip Simmons uncovers hard-to-find and vintage items for her little shop, Miss Mae's. In the home-design section upstairs, you'll unearth linen sheets alongside exotic Balinese and French furniture that she buys one piece at a time. India Hicks, who also owns the Landing hotel nearby, runs the Sugar Mill Trading Company, an eclectic space that's all palm-print wallpaper, finely lacquered woods, and furniture upholstered in David Hicks fabric. The stock includes beachwear by her good friend Elizabeth Hurley, Bollywood-inspired caftans by Sita de Vesci, and Erica Weiner charm necklaces trimmed in copper and brass. The shop may embody Harbour Island's singular style better than any other. +

For The Guide, see page 267.

The Baptistery at the church of El Santuario de Atotonilco in San Miguel de Allende.

MEXICO + CENTRAL + SOUTH AMERICA

GLOBAL VILLAGE

A Melding of Cultures in San Miguel de Allende

FOR MORE THAN 70 YEARS, EXPATRIATES have moved to San Miguel de Allende, in the green highlands of the central Mexican state of Guanajuato, to reinvent their lives. They own cafés, bakeries, guesthouses, clothing stores, art galleries, language schools, day spas, and bars. They teach cooking classes, arrange traditional weddings

~La Parroquia church, which crowns the town of San Miguel de Allende.

(for non-Mexicans), and lead architectural tours. They publish a newspaper, an art magazine, and a telephone directory for expatriates.

San Miguel has witnessed a remarkable transformation in recent years: a pair of big shopping centers are being built on the edge of town, two high-end international hotel chains are entering the market, and houses that had sold for tens of thousands five years ago are now going for millions.

But the city still maintains its unique spirit and a sense of intimacy, thanks in part to the fact that it's somewhat remote, on a mesa almost four hours by car from Mexico City. The narrow cobblestoned streets are surrounded by high stucco walls in shades of red (cayenne, rust, clay). In the central plaza—called El Jardín— people sit on benches beneath small trees, where the leaves have been clipped into geometric boxes, and a woman sells *elotes* (roasted ears of corn). The parish church, La Parroquia, is as grand and fanciful as Gaudí's Sagrada Familia in Barcelona, but here, rather than melt, the architecture soars, the rose-colored spires flaming against the deep blue sky.

From the Jardín, it's an easy stroll to Benito Juárez Park, a small French-style garden that was recently restored for its 100th birthday. El Chorro, the town's waterworks and public laundry, is next to the park. The tubs look like a sculptured fountain, but Mexican women still come to wash clothes in them, and you may occasionally see a thirsty horse drinking.

In some ways, San Miguel hasn't

changed much since the 1930's, when José Mojica, a Mexican opera singer and movie star, discovered the town. Back then, it was a ruin, full of fantastical churches and empty mansions. Mojica told friends about his find, and others soon joined him, including Chilean poets Gabriela Mistral and Pablo Neruda, and Felipe Cossío del Pomar, a Peruvian writer who founded the Escuela de Bellas Artes (School of Fine Arts) in 1938. The school's American director, Stirling Dickinson, advertised Bellas Artes in the United States as a place where vets on the GI Bill could study and live in relative style. Dickinson later cofounded an arts-and-language school, the Instituto Allende, which drew international students well into the 1980's.

Although neither school is the economic catalyst it once was, without them San Miguel might have been very different from what it is today—a quiet historic artifact turned cosmopolitan center, populated by people like Detlev Kappstein, who owns the Berlin Bar & Café. Like the most relaxed of hosts at a private party, Kappstein has as much fun as anyone else in the arty crowd of Americans, Europeans, and Mexicans. And then there's Sylvia Samuelson, who can often be found standing in her doorway on the central plaza, watching the life of the town around her. She arrived in 1952, when there were only 40 expats, and opened the city's first gallery, Galería San Miguel, in 1962. After more than 50 years here, she remains fascinated by this place. +

For The Guide, see page 268.

The Rico family of mariachis on the central plaza, El Jardín, left. Above: Berlin Bar & Café. Opposite: Outside the Escuela de Bellas Artes.

BAJA FRESH

**The Resort-Filled
Playground of Los Cabos**

The reception area of Las Ventanas al Paraíso, in Cabo San Lucas, left. Below: Las Ventanas's infinity pool. Opposite: Snorkeling off Santa Maria Bay in Cabo San Lucas, Mexico.

IN 1940, JOHN STEINBECK VENTURED ON AN EXPEDITION to Baja California, the peninsula off Mexico's west coast; he found more signs of life in the tidal pools than on land. Locals still refer to Baja as *La Frontera* ("the frontier") because it remains largely undeveloped—except for the peninsula's tip, where the area known as Los Cabos ("the capes") is booming and you can find half of Hollywood sneaking down for a break.

The port town of Cabo San Lucas is a nonstop fiesta, packed with souvenir stalls and theme bars. Twenty miles away, colonial San José del Cabo clings tenaciously to its Mexican roots; narrow side streets reveal sleepy cantinas and folk-art boutiques. The corridor between the two towns is lined with beaches, golf courses, and a heavy concentration of glitzy resorts.

What the lavish, 56-room Esperanza lacks in shoreline—it has two tiny coves—the resort compensates for with rare tequila tastings, Baja lime–scented bath products, and a spa illuminated by candles after dusk.

Down the coast, the vibe is muted Mex-Med at Las Ventanas al Paraíso ("windows to paradise"), which has 61 sprawling suites equipped with telescopes for stargazing.

And at One & Only Palmilla, there's a Charlie Trotter restaurant and a fleet of butlers delivering loaded iPods to the captains of industry reclining poolside. ✦

For The Guide, see page 268.

Harvesting a ripe agave heart, along Jalisco's tequila trail, west of Mexico City, left. Below: Bottles of tequila at the Mundo Cuervo distillery.

MEXICAN GOLD
Following Jalisco's Tequila Trail

IN THE AGAVE FIELDS OF JALISCO, 350 miles west of Mexico City, a new generation of distillers is focusing on premium, artisanal tequila. Along the state's Tequila Trail—between the towns of Tequila and Arandas—more than 146 distilleries produce 50 million gallons a year. But it's the rare stuff, the Mexican equivalent of a single-malt, that's worth hunting for.

Many of the best batches can be found in the town of Tequila, where the scent of roasting agave (a spiny succulent used to make the drink) permeates the air. Sip a delicate six-year-old *añejo* from a flute at the old-fashioned El Llano, where fifth-generation distillers craft their label Arette (restricted to 25,000 cases annually). Nearby Los Abuelos brews just 300 cases; their sweet *blanco* is mild and fruity. At Mundo Cuervo, you'll find a margarita bar and the distillery La Rojeña. Recently, Juan Beckmann,

a descendant of José Cuervo, released 600 cases of Maestro Tequilero *añejo*, made from agave harvested when the sugars in the plant are concentrated. The flavor notes are brazenly hot.

Travel to Las Altos, Jalisco's other major tequila district, and visit Siete Leguas to view the fermentation vats, brimming with yeasty liquid. Be sure to pick up a bottle of their *añejo*, which is as smooth as Cognac. You may have come for a lesson in tequila, but you'll leave with the nation's pride and joy. ✚

For The Guide, see page 268.

STILL WATERS

Aquatic Pursuits in Placencia

WEDGED BETWEEN GUATEMALA AND MEXICO'S Yucatán Peninsula, Belize is a favorite destination for adventure travelers. It's an unspoiled land of lush mountains and jungles, pristine Caribbean beaches and islands, and the longest barrier reef in the Western Hemisphere. Placencia, a 16-mile-long peninsula off the coast with hippie cafés and funky guesthouses, is like the Caribbean circa 1968.

Stay at the Inn at Robert's Grove, with a thatched dock jutting out into the sea. The hotel runs guided trips in the neighboring lagoon to see manatees. Or charter a catamaran from the Moorings, and skim over the turquoise sea to the countless islands that dot the calm, reef-protected waters. An hour away, Laughing Bird Caye is an ideal place to drop anchor and start spotting angelfish or colorful coral—even whale sharks, which are harmless to humans, despite being a menacing 65 feet long. **✛**

For The Guide, see page 268.

The Inn at Robert's Grove in Placencia, on Belize's central coast.

Bogotá's main cathedral, which dates from the 16th century.

BOGOTÁ ANEW

Rediscovering Colombia's Capital

T+L Tip

The State Department has issued a travel warning for Colombia and strongly discourages visitors from going to rural areas. See travel.state.gov for more details. It's advisable to book trips through a travel agent, such as Douglas Wren at PanAmerican Travel Services (800/364-4359; panam-tours.com).

FOR DECADES BOGOTÁ WAS UNDER VIRTUAL SIEGE, victim of a civil war. But the relative calm of recent years has helped attract foreign visitors back to the Colombian capital.

On the northern edge of town, defense contractors linger on the patio of the Bogotá Beer Company. Nearby, posh lounges and casinos teem with *traquetos*: millionaires who drive black SUV's and are trailed by an entourage of *cuchibarbies*—Barbies by the plastic surgeon's knife.

Bogotá's real charm lies in La Candelaria, a recently revitalized district of grand colonial buildings and narrow cobblestoned streets. The neighborhood is home to Bolívar Square—dating back to the 16th century—and the Teatro Colón, which hosts one of the continent's top theater festivals. Restored mansions have been turned into museums, while galleries, yoga studios, and dimly lit cafés give the area an air of gentrifying boho-chic. ✚

For The Guide, see page 268.

JUNGLE FEVER

A Journey in the Peruvian Amazon

A waterfront trailhead in Peru's Amazon rain forest.

SURE, IT'S STEAMY AND BUGGY, BUT THE Amazon is a worthy frontier, untamed and incompletely understood. For anyone who loves exotic animals, the rain forest delivers in limitless variety.

Luckily, it's not hard to reach; from Lima, take an 80-minute flight to the river town of Puerto Maldonado and watch from the plane as the snow-capped Andes quickly drop off into a sea of green that is the rain forest. The

Scarlet macaws, above. Right: The broadleaf maidenhair fern, which makes a ghostly tattoo.Opposite: Hanging around the Tambopata Research Center.

tributaries of the Amazon are the traditional roads in this part of the world. One of them, the Tambopata, links to the wilderness.

From the village known as Infierno—that's right, Hell—a vessel will take you downriver to the Posada Amazonas lodge. Along the way, a primordial landscape of high-tree canopies drifts by. Surprising creatures emerge: weaverbirds with forked tails; black caracara raptors; and families of the world's largest rodent, the capybara. River parasites—as well as piranhas, caimans, and unexpected currents—make swimming ill-advised.

The roofs of the main structure of the Posada Amazonas are churchlike in angle, high beams supporting traditional thatch. Everything is on stilts to keep it away from bugs. Walkways lead to 30 guest rooms, each with one side open to the forest, beds under mosquito nets, and so many candles you barely notice the lack of electricity.

Hikes in the rain forest are an experience of enclosure. The canopy obscures the sky and the air is still. You're in a world of spaced-apart trunks, low shrubs, and fallen branches. You get the feeling that there are plenty of animals and unusual flora around; the challenge is finding them. There are titi monkeys, toucans, and ferns with leaves that, when pressed against the skin, leave a white tattoo.

A five-hour boat ride brings you to Rainforest Expedition's Tambopata

Entering the Amazon rain forest, near the Tambopata Research Center.

THE ROUTE TO MACHU PICCHU

Combine a trip to the Amazon with a visit to Peru's Machu Picchu, a set of 15th-century ruins that were unearthed in 1911. The lost city is a maze of paths, partly standing granite buildings, and stone steps on a remote Andean ridge 7,790 feet above the sea.

Getting There Start in Cuzco, a thriving colonial city 44 miles south of the ruins (it's a one-hour flight from Lima). From there it's a four-hour train ride to the town of Aguas Calientes, 15 minutes by bus from the site.

Staying There Just outside of town, the 85-room Machu Picchu Pueblo Hotel sits in a cloud forest. Or splurge on the Machu Picchu Sanctuary Lodge, right outside the gates to the ruins.

Research Center (TRC). A scaled-down version of Posada Amazonas, TRC has 13 dorm-size bedrooms. The center started up in 1989, and its research station began hosting small numbers of tourists in 1992. Tourism helps fund the fieldwork, most of which involves macaws. TRC is located near what is said to be the world's largest macaw clay lick—a cliffside at which the birds eat the dirt they need to stay healthy. Visitors here can witness an impressive mass visitation of up to 1,500 birds.

Another highlight is a night outing. A guide shines a light into the water, revealing dozens of pairs of caiman eyes. Along an embankment, the darkness glows with the bioluminescence of firefly larvae. Next, slog around in the swamp, with lights out, waiting for the inhabitants to reveal themselves with barks and peeps. Lights on, you'll spot them astride twigs and leaves: rain frogs, hyla frogs, monkey frogs. An owl hoots. A bat brushes by. When the Amazon is right for you, it's very, very right. +

For The Guide, see page 269.

The hills of Colchagua Valley, south of Santiago, right. Below: The Clos Apalta Winery.

VINTAGE CHILE

A Wine Country Tour

T+L Tip

For additional information, including current Chilean wine news and links to specific wineries, see winesofchile.cl, or planetavino.com.

WINERY-HOPPING IN CHILE once meant exhausting day trips from Santiago. But with the opening of guesthouses and restaurants in the Aconcagua and Colchagua valleys, 90 minutes from downtown Santiago, a tasting tour couldn't be easier.

The ride to 136-year-old Viña Errázuriz, in Aconcagua, traces the Andean foothills. The finale of the two-hour estate visit is a sampling of rare Sangioveses, Pinots, and Shirazes. Scenic Route 60 then winds down along the Aconcagua River toward Viña Matetic, a small winery making big waves in organic production. Drop your bags at the guesthouse before exploring the valley on horseback or bicycle. Move on to Apalta, 100 miles south, in the Colchagua Valley. French owner Alexandra Marnier Lapostolle produces the premium line of Casa Lapostolle at the Clos Apalta Winery, which also has four luxurious bungalows to rent. From your private deck, the views of the vine-ruffled hills are as spectacular as the wine itself. ✚

For The Guide, see page 269.

UNDER THE SPELL

The Ancient Stone Sentinels of Easter Island

THE JOURNEY TO EASTER ISLAND feels like sailing over the edge of the earth. The plane leaves Santiago at dusk and chases the setting sun. For five hours, you fly west across one of the emptiest expanses of ocean on the planet—thousands of miles of lightly ruffled blue, not a scrap of land in sight. Suddenly, just as you wonder if the plane is going to run out of fuel, a green form rears from the deep like a sea monster, craning its long neck forward, its humped body behind. It is the island.

Rapa Nui, as the natives have called this land mass since long before a Dutch ship sighted it on Easter Sunday, 1722, is about the size of Staten Island—but the thousands of miles that separate it from the next human settlement magnify its size many times over. Rapa Nui exerts a disproportionately strong

A row of *moai* at Ahu
Tongariki, on Easter Island,
off the coast of Chile.

Local resident Lucas Camus dressed for festivities in Hanga Roa, Easter Island's capital, above left. Above right: The view of Ahu at Tongariki.

magnetic pull on the imagination of the outside world. Once you're on land and glancing over the green hillocks strewn with black boulders, it isn't hard to discern why. The high, nearly tree-less meadows slope toward dark bluffs where the surf thrashes and sighs. Then you see, lying on its back in the tall grass, a toppled giant of volcanic stone, its eroded eye sockets gaping sightlessly at the sky. It is one of the island's nearly one thousand statues known as *moai*, some of which are more than 30 feet high and weigh as much as 20 tons. You'll immediately understand why people talk of space aliens and why the modern-day Easter Islanders—descendants of the statues' builders—insist that the *moai* walked on their own across the island. The most remark-able thing about the statues is that they are profound works of art. It's as if they are the original human sculptures, of which everything else—from ancient Greek kouroi to Christo's Central Park *Gates*—is a copy.

With angular faces, the people themselves seem to be part *moai*. The culture appears to be poised between the pre-historic and the postmodern. Inhabitants know enough to be

Playing pool at the Hotel Hanga Roa, above left. Above right: The tattoo on "Silver" Silvestre, a surfer who lives in Hanga Roa.

impressed by famous visitors (such as one of the creators of *The Simpsons*), yet when islanders take off their Western clothes at palm-fringed beaches, they reveal tattoos of ancestral gods. At the Hotel Hanga Roa, they dance to Polynesian music with a bluegrass rhythm, and sweaty crowds party at seaside discos.

The longer you stay on the island, the more you are drawn back to one spot: Rano Raraku. At the crater of the extinct volcano, stone was quarried over a thousand years ago for the colossal *moai*, most of which were then moved and set up as sentries on stone platforms ringing the coast. Though the *moai* on the shoreline platforms were toppled by later generations of islanders, those at Rano Raraku were allowed to stand.

Here, you can have one of the great places on earth to yourself. Wander among the statues until long after sunset, watching the monoliths in the changing light. The only sign of life might be the occasional frigate bird sailing overhead. Afternoon gives way to sunset, blue dusk, then night, and you leave the statues, standing glyphlike, solitary against the sky. ✢

For The Guide, see page 269.

A view of Argentina's
Mount Fitz Roy, in
Patagonia. Opposite,
from left: A horse at
Eolo, a hotel in southern
Argentina; The pool
at Remota, in Chile.

THE WILD SOUTH
Hiking Through Patagonia

PATAGONIA IS MYTHICAL, a place that lives as much in the imagination as in reality. Covering about 260,000 square miles, it spans a significant portion of lower South America. The name alone conjures images of spiky peaks, endless steppes, and glaciers that tumble into electric-blue lakes. And now, a clutch of stylish lodges are making previously unexplored areas accessible.

Near El Calafate, 455 miles above the tip of the continent, Eolo is the best hotel in southern Argentina. People come here to see ice: the Southern Patagonian Ice Field, and the Perito Moreno and Upsala glaciers. Behind the hotel, you can hike the Cerro Frijas; on a clear day you'll see Torres del Paine, in Chile.

Several hours north, in El Chaltén, Los Cerros is a luxury hostel offering exceptional treks. Climb to the shore of Laguna de los Tres, a glacial lake in the shadow of Mount Fitz Roy, then along a red-rock ridge above the Río de Las Vueltas. Afterwards, sink your feet into the cool pebbles at Capri Lagoon.

Outside Puerto Natales, in Chile, Remota is a dazzling project from Germán del Sol, the Chilean architect who designed several properties owned by hotel-adventure company Explora. Guests here get to see a complete picture of Patagonia. One hike leads visitors to the remote Sierra Baguales, where they have lunch with a cowboy who has lived alone in this valley for 20 years. ✦

For The Guide, see page 269.

A candomblé ceremony, in Salvador, left. Below: On Porto da Barra, a popular beach. Opposite: The main square in the Pelourinho neighborhood.

AFRICAN SOUL
Salvador's Cultural Heritage

THE FIRST COLONIAL CAPITAL OF BRAZIL and now a city of more than 2 million inhabitants, Salvador juts into the Bay of All Saints. But in reality, the *baia* is just preliminary, for Salvador stretches clear across the Atlantic to the heart of Yoruba culture, into modern-day Nigeria, Benin, and Togo. The food is bathed in palm oil, an African staple. The popular mode of prayer is candomblé, a fusion of Catholic rites and elaborate ceremonies centered on offerings. When you're watching a performance of capoeira Angola—a mixture of nonviolent martial arts, interactive ballet, and musical comedy—or biting into a fritter filled with black-eyed peas, Brazil can seem more African than Africa itself.

Most visits start in the Upper City neighborhood called the Pelourinho, which means "the Pillory." It's perched high atop a 236-foot-high bluff overlooking the bay, the sunburned Lower City, and the favelas, or shantytowns, that are as poor as any place on earth, clinging impossibly to eroding hills, oddly attractive from a distance, spirit-shattering when seen up close. Pelourinho's streets slope down without warning, then ramp up into the sky. One minute the bulbous spires of the Igreja de Nossa Senhora do Rosário dos Pretos are at your feet; the next, you're staring up at the sky-blue façade of the

A view from the Lacerda elevator, which connects Salvador's Upper City to the harbor, above. Left: A girl at a Salvador school.

church, built for slaves, by slaves, and still bursting with the sounds of the Yoruba-language mass.

On the main square of Terreiro de Jesus, visit the Museu Afro-Brasileiro, which gives a good overview of the unique Afrocentric culture of Bahia (Salvador's state), touching upon the three C's: candomblé, capocira, and the Carnaval, said to rival Rio's. Some residents, however, bemoan a slide into commercialization.

After a few days in Pelourinho's stunning colonial wonderland, you'll look forward to seeing the rest of the city. In Salvador's outskirts, acolytes of candomblé clad in Bahian white dance to the beat of drums and an undulating Yoruba chant. There are beaches where locals parade their flesh, and samba places where they shake it.

At the bar O Cravinho, dapper gentlemen and the occasional over-soused foreigner trade conversation and clink caipirinhas. In the rear, at Fundo do Cavinho (which means "Back of O Cavinho"), a hangar-like space with blue plastic chairs, the drink of choice is a tall dark bottle of ice-cold beer, and hip-hugging couples dance with minute precision, as if their lives depended on it. ✦

For The Guide, see page 269.

Designer
Tufi Duek at
a fitting in
his São Paulo
studio.

FASHION FORWARD

**World-Class
Shopping in São Paulo**

GOLDEN SAND, JIGGLING SAMBA QUEENS in rhinestone
nothings, and a bossa nova singer's coo: so goes the
standard travelogue of Brazil. But the chaotic city of
São Paulo is a far more engaging place, full of creativity,
sprawl, and electric contradiction. Thanks to the
cross-pollination of cultures—including the biggest

A view of downtown São Paulo, left. Below: The four-story Clube Chocolate. Opposite: Tufi Duek's Forum boutique.

Japanese enclave outside of Japan—São Paulo is closer to being a world capital than a Latin American one.

Style plays an important part in the mix. São Paulo's two fashion weeks, which take place in January and June, rival the World Cup in Brazilian TV ratings. There's a raft of excellent designers who have had little exposure in the United States.

The city's Santa Marcelina fashion school encourages independence: since the first class graduated in 1991, the impulse to knock off the Europeans has weakened with every season. Now, but for a few exceptions, the clothes at Clube Chocolate, a four-story shop featuring minimalist wood interiors on Rua Oscar Freire (São Paulo's answer to Rodeo Drive), are all Brazilian. At his Forum boutique, designer Tufi Duek—one of Brazil's best-selling exports—shares space with evening-gown king Carlos Miele.

No trip to the city would be complete without a visit to the famous Daslu and its 25,000 square feet of boutiques selling everything from cars to Chanel (a big new section is dedicated to Brazilian talent). Housed in a contemporary high-rise with a rooftop helipad, Daslu has helped many a daughter of Latin America's robber barons haul home the Gucci. ✛

For The Guide, see page 269.

WESTERN EUROPE

Place Charles de Gaulle, also known as the Grande Place, in Lille, France.

LONDON CALLING

A Guide to the Thriving Contemporary Art Scene

Stuart Shave, owner of East London's Modern Art gallery, with artist Lara Schnitger. Opposite, from top: Anselm Kiefer's Jericho towers, a site-specific installation at the Royal Academy of Arts; bronze sculptures from *When Humans Walked the Earth*, 2006, by Jake and Dinos Chapman at Tate Britain.

IN THE ART WORLD OF THE MOMENT,
Britannia rules. Once considered a
backwater of old-master dealers, London is now a powerhouse, with more
creative and commercial clout than
any place outside of New York. The
world's most influential galleries, such
as Gagosian in New York and Zurich's
Hauser & Wirth, have opened outposts
in the British capital. Dozens of new
spaces have surfaced in edgy East London. And every October, international
collectors flood the city for the Frieze
Art Fair, organized by the London-
based international art journal *Frieze*,
codirected by Matthew Slotover.

A decade ago, all this would have
been inconceivable. "Things were very
different in the early 1990's," reminisces
New York–born Maureen Paley, who
moved to London in 1977 and is now
one of its leading gallerists. "There was
no contemporary art scene as such."
The city has long had great museums
with imposing historic collections and
scholarly exhibitions, but the avant-
garde was relegated to publicly funded
exhibition spaces like the Whitechapel,
Serpentine, and Hayward galleries.
There were very few contemporary art
collectors and certainly no world-class
contemporary art fair.

Today, London's storied institu-
tions—the National Gallery, National
Portrait Gallery, Victoria and Albert
Museum, the British Museum, the
Royal Academy of Arts, Tate Britain,

Birdshit Paintings, 2007, by Dan Colen, in a
group show at the Victoria Miro Gallery
in East London. Opposite: The White Cube's
East End gallery in Hoxton Square.

and Tate Modern—all have peerless
permanent collections and mount
exhibits of international stature, such
as the V&A's recent exploration of
surrealism and design. Comparably
diverse exhibitions are on view at
smaller public art institutions, such as
the Hayward Gallery in South Bank
and the Whitechapel Gallery in East
London. And every July, Londoners
look forward to the summer pavilion
in Hyde Park, an annual architecture
commission by the Serpentine Gallery,
which in the past has been designed

by names like Rem Koolhaas, Danish conceptual artist Olafur
Eliasson, and Norwegian architect Kjetil Thorsen.

Commercial galleries are the latest additions to the art
scene. One is the space opened by the German dealers Monika
Sprüth and Philomene Magers in an 18th-century building
on Grafton Street in Mayfair. Nearby is White Cube's
new gallery, a glass-topped box in the middle of Mason's Yard.
At Coppermill, its project space in East London, Hauser &
Wirth presents ambitious shows, such as works by the Turner
Prize–winning British conceptual artist Martin Creed.

London now has two distinct gallery districts: the tony West
End and the rapidly gentrifying East End. Neither is as
concentrated geographically as, say, Chelsea in New York, but
together they can be easily covered in a day. Gagosian, Sadie

Coles, Hauser & Wirth, and the rest of the "new establishment" have set up shop in the West End's Piccadilly and Mayfair. The smaller, more experimental galleries—along with a few big ones—are camped in abandoned warehouses in the East End, mostly clustered around Hoxton Square and Herald and Vyner streets. Here you'll find Stuart Shave/Modern Art, which features rising talent like sculptor Lara Schnitger and urban installation specialist Barry McGee.

Even if they're not one of the heavyweight collectors on Larry Gagosian's speed dial, art enthusiasts are pulled into the whirl. "London has everything—great museums, great galleries, and great artists," says Matthew Slotover, codirector of the *Frieze* art fair. "There's an amazing range of shows on at any one time." +

For The Guide, see page 270.

ART WORLD OUTPOSTS

Where to go in London when you need a break from gallery hopping.

Eat

Bistrotheque A converted factory in Hackney, with white walls, an exposed ceiling, and a top-notch bistro menu.

Scott's Fantastic artwork, such as a fish-and-crustacean display, adorns the walls of this seafood restaurant in Mayfair.

St. John Beloved by the art world in Clerkenwell for offbeat dishes, like pigs' trotters and tripe. The atmosphere is suggestive of its days as a smokehouse.

Drink

BoomBox Sundays at this Hoxton Square party pulse with the energy of the new rave music scene.

Golden Heart With Adnams Bitter and Broadside on tap, this comfy Spitalfields spot is a long-standing watering hole for Britain's art crowd.

Sleep

Brown's Hotel Collectors consider the elegant Mayfair hotel a second home.

Shop

Dover Street Market Emerging designers coexist with known brands in this six-floor shop in Mayfair devoted to avant-garde clothing, art, and design.

London's bustling Borough Market, underneath Victorian railway arches, right. Below: Apples for sale at the market.

TO BOROUGH MARKET
London's Top Food Destination

ON FRIDAYS AND SATURDAYS, organic farmers, bakers, and importers fill the stalls of London's Borough Market, at the London Bridge tube stop, turning the streets into a gourmet haven.

It's worth braving the line for the juicy venison burgers sizzling on the grill at Westcountry Venison. For fresh-pressed olive oils and cured meats, go to Brindisa Spanish Foods. The market's purveyors come only on weekends, but some goods are available at the area's permanent shops and stalls. Nigella Lawson is a fan of the moist cakes at Konditor & Cook. And Neal's Yard Dairy is a temple to cheese with a massive open counter, and 50 varieties on display, including British all-stars such as Montgomery's Cheddar and Colston Bassett Stilton.

Stalls and shops are joined by restaurants with farm-fresh food. Roast, a glass-enclosed space in Floral Hall, packs seasonal ingredients into British dishes. Set under Victorian railway arches, Brew Wharf pairs house ales with solid brasserie fare such as braised pork belly and red cabbage. And the oysters at Wright Brothers Oyster & Porter House come straight from the Prince of Wales's farm in Cornwall. ✚

For The Guide, see page 270.

A GARDEN TOUR

An Oasis in Northumberland

FROM THE 18TH CENTURY ON, ALNWICK Castle, located in northeast England's Northumberland county, had distinguished gardens. In fact, in the 19th century, Czar Alexander I of Russia so admired Alnwick's hothouses and conservatories during a visit that he poached the head gardener and took him back to St. Petersburg. But by the 1950's, the garden that had once supplied pineapples

Jane Percy, the Duchess of Northumberland, at Alnwick Garden, in England.

On the grounds of Alnwick Castle in Northumberland, left. Above: A dove house at the castle. Opposite: The walled Ornamental Garden, with 16,500 European plants.

to the British ambassador in Paris had fallen into disrepair. Enter the Duchess of Northumberland, Jane Percy, who has transformed the garden's 40 acres—at an estimated cost of $70 million—into one of the most ambitious horticultural projects in Europe since Versailles.

The first thing you will notice is the water. Walk through the new pavilion and visitors' center and you'll see the Grand Cascade: 21 weirs, down which tumble 8,700 gallons of water per minute. It's the beginning of a series of water sculptures that punctuate the space. A little farther on is *Torricelli*, one of eight pieces by British artist William Pye. The 16-foot-high stainless-steel column slowly fills until it overflows down the mirrorlike sides. *Vortex*, also by Pye, resembles a stainless-steel shaving bowl. As water flows in, vents send it into diverging directions, creating a vortex.

The Ornamental Garden, with its 16,500 plants, was originally used as a nursery to supply trees for the duke's estates. Today, it is a riot of color, with chest-high delphiniums, roses, and dozens of varieties of perennials.

Alnwick even has its own restaurant—one that ideally suits the setting. It's a giant tree house, 6,000 square feet of cedar, Scandinavian redwood, and English and Scotch pine, held aloft by 17 lime trees. ✛

For The Guide, see page 271.

BEST BREADS

Sampling the Boulangeries of Paris

WHEN IT COMES TO BAGUETTES AND croissants, it's no surprise that the French capital delivers. In addition to the ultimate brioche, you'll find heavenly twists on classics, too.

Start with breakfast at Boulangerie Bechu, a striking Art Deco shop where the *retro d'or ficelle*, a skinny variation on baguettes, is at its best when paired with apricot jam and *café crème*.

A Grand Prix winner of the Best Baguette in Paris award, Gosselin's Philippe Gosselin has supplied his classic loaves—made from white flour, sea salt, and leavening—to the Elysée Palace. At world-famous Poilâne, bread is still baked in an antique wood-fired oven. The big, round *miche*, a dense sourdough loaf made from stone-ground flour, can be decorated to your specifications.

The template for the ultimate brioche is found at La Flûte Gana where the *vendéenne* is buttery, with a hint of fresh vanilla. Since no tour would be complete without a croissant, pick one up at La Maison Kayser. Baker Eric Kayser's croissants are decadently plump, with a meltingly tender center and a golden exterior that flakes at the merest touch. ✛

For The Guide, see page 271.

Outside Poilâne in Paris, where bread is baked in a wood-fired oven, top left. Left: Fresh-from-the-oven baguettes at Gosselin.

RIDE OF A LIFETIME

Bicycle Through Versailles

VERSAILLES IS 20 MINUTES AWAY FROM PARIS by cab and three-and-a-half centuries away in time. Grandiose and overwhelming, it stands for everything pompous about France. In 1661, Louis XIV took over a marsh west of Paris to build the best palace in the world. The Revolution trashed the place, but then, for two centuries, punctilious curators reassembled the treasures while gardeners snipped and seeded the grounds.

Versailles has the hidden bounty of a magical, carefully tended 17th-century park, whose dimensions and details exceed the reach of any map or guidebook. The grounds were meant to be experienced on horseback, but on a bike, you can ride for hours without seeing a trace of today. A bicycle is lower than a horse, but it never shies, bucks, or needs water, and when you look up as you pedal along, the carefully trimmed

Biking past Versailles's Grand Canal

The formal gardens designed by Le Nôtre, at Versailles, left. Above: Picking wildflowers in the fields beyond Versailles's Allée de Bally. Opposite: One of Versailles's entrance gates.

trees unfold in perfect symmetry above your head, and the subtle Pythagorean perfections of French ideals realign you into harmony.

You can rent large, sturdy bicycles at an entrance gate called the Grille de la Reine, on the east side of the park. From there, it's a direct shot to the Grand Canal. Veering right, the trees race staccato on the left, and the water is bounded by a white stone ledge just beyond.

The first right turn on the cross-shaped canal leads to the side of the Grand Trianon. Ride past the Fer à Cheval fountain and into the Allée de Bally, where the straight line of trees is suddenly brushed with long grasses, the shade is thicker, and strollers and other bikers immediately vanish.

At the end of the Allée de Bally is virgin countryside: fields of wildflowers as far as the eye can see. Just beyond a tall wall is the Ferme de Gally, where children can pet goats and learn all about aubergines and apples. Pedal along the southern edge of the Grand Canal, and you'll arrive at the gates that separate the formal gardens, designed by Le Nôtre, from the larger park. Ride through them and around the Bassin d'Apollon, and you'll find a shack that sells miniature reproductions of Versailles clocks, tiny ornate slippers rendered in painted resin, and a much-deserved bottle of mineral water. +

For The Guide, see page 271.

COUNTRY TABLES

A Culinary Tour of Provence Bistros

Grilled vegetables at La Charcuterie, in Arles.

The courtyard at Le Jardin du Quai, in L'Isle-sur-la-Sorgue, left. Above: A bowl of Provence-grown figs.

IN THE FRENCH COUNTRYSIDE, nothing compares to a multi-course dinner, but the noon-to-three-o'clock slice of the day provides the perfect opportunity for leisurely lunches, with fresh-from-the-market ingredients. The best bistros in Provence possess four basic characteristics: a distinct personality, intimacy, a convivial atmosphere, and a generous spirit.

The owners of La Charcuterie, in Arles, wanted to create a *bistro des copains* (bistro for friends), as they put it, and they succeeded. The winsome space has a modest décor of red-velvet banquettes and pig figurines. And with main courses featuring Charolais beef and grilled duck, the menu is a carnivore's dream.

Even with its Michelin two-star rating and refined interior, the Bistrot d'Eygalières has maintained the true appeal of a bis-

tro while offering a menu of exquisitely nuanced regional cuisine. A lunch at this *bistro de luxe*, located in a village a few miles south of the road between St.-Rémy and Cavaillon, might include a crisply grilled fillet of baby pig and a "gazpacho" of fragrant strawberries.

The former Avignon mansion of Jules Pernod, creator of the liqueur of the same name, now houses Numéro 75. Set behind an iron gate, 75 feels like a secret garden, fragrant with mimosa, bougainvillea, and lemon. The menus

A lunch spread at La Chassagnette, south of Arles, right. Above: Near the village of Eygalières. Opposite: Inside La Charcuterie.

are short, with only a handful of choices, such as pan-roasted guinea hen and tangy lemon confit.

East of Avignon lies L'Isle-sur-la-Sorgue, a riverside town of antiques shops and Le Jardin du Quai, one of the best restaurants to open in Provence in the past five years. The simple but sophisticated market-based menu (cod fillet, a poached peach in sugar syrup) is served in a retro atmosphere, complete with an old zinc bar and vintage tables.

In the tourist-clogged town of Gordes, it's not easy finding authentic, reasonably priced food. The crab tartare and summer greens at Le Bouquet de Basilic, tucked behind a souvenir shop, are adorable discoveries. Many dishes include the owner's fresh basil, which lends its name to the restaurant, as well as house-grown garlic and locally pressed olive oil.

The quintessential small-town bistro is in Apt. At Bistro de France, meals are good the way the best home cooking is: fresh, unadorned, and generously served. With seasonal specials and menu classics like *blanquette de veau*—a creamy veal stew that's the ultimate bistro comfort food—it's no surprise Bistro de France always plays to a full house. ✚

For The Guide, see page 271.

Bonbons at Méert, a 1761 confectioner in Lille, top. Above: Dinner in the 18th-century rooms of La Petite Cour. Opposite: The cobblestoned Rue Lepelletier, in Lille's Old City.

LILLE LIFE

Quintessential France in the Old Flemish City

JUST AN HOUR BY TRAIN FROM PARIS, Lille, the former capital of Flanders, delightfully marries the best of Belgian and French traditions.

Since 1761, one of France's oldest confectioners, Méert, has occupied a spun-sugar rococo tea room on the Place Charles de Gaulle, known as the Grande Place. (Don't miss their exquisitely packaged bonbons—you won't find them outside the city.) Although artisanal bread and pastry maker Paul, which was founded in Lille in 1889, has expanded its empire as far as Dubai and Palm Beach, the cozy, Delft-tiled bakery on the Rue de Paris still serves creamy, thick hot chocolate. And locals have long been congregating in the warren of 18th-century rooms and alcoves at La Petite Cour for home-country fare such as *sole meunière*.

For a relatively small-town venue, the opera house, L'Opéra de Lille, has long attracted eminences to its Beaux-Arts stage; Merce Cunningham, among others, has performed here. But traditionalists will relish viewing classics like *La Traviata*.

Historically, one of Lille's only drawbacks was a dearth of stylish hotels. L'Hermitage Gantois, in a 15th-century former hospice, has changed all that. Admire the hotel's Flemish architectural details in the brick atrium, and the perfectly manicured rose gardens in the cloisters. ✚

For The Guide, see page 271.

A canal in downtown Ghent, Belgium.

PAINTED PAST

An Art Tour of Belgium

PERHAPS THE BEST WAY TO UNDERSTAND the peculiarity of Belgium is to look at the history of its art. Painting, more than anything, is the glory of the country. From Rubens to Magritte, the dreams of the nation have been recorded on canvas and wood, and through them runs a thread of the surreal, which might contain the key to what Belgium is about.

A perfectly preserved medieval city, Bruges, near the northwest coast, is one of those rare places where you can look out the window of a museum and see more or less what the old masters saw. Not only is the 14th-century town hall still there, but the old streets remain intact. The wealth and elegance of Bruges from 1384 to the late 15th century, when it was ruled by the dukes of Burgundy, can be experienced in the masterpieces by Jan van Eyck. One now hangs in the Groeninge Museum. Painted in 1436, it shows the Madonna and Child sitting on a throne. The eye is drawn less to the piety of the scene than to the opulence of the setting: the marble columns, the richly worked

The Memling Museum in Bruges, located in a former medieval hospital.

throne, the Persian carpets, the silk upholstery, the brocade rugs.

Like Bruges, Antwerp, about 50 miles east, once regarded itself as the center of the world. Pieter Brueghel the Elder painted *The Tower of Babel* here in 1563, when Antwerp was at the height of its power. A building boom had made the city one of the largest in Europe, with more than 100,000 inhabitants. Merchants from all over flocked to Bruges, trading in many

languages. Today, you can tour the building where Peter Paul Rubens lived, which is now a museum. Built in 1610, the house is Flemish Baroque at its best, filled with such beautiful pieces as the artist's sketch of the Annunciation and his self-portrait, which hangs in the Renaissance-style dining room. His paintings explored Flemish secular excess, with pink cherubs and fat mortals enjoying fleshly delights. The surprise of Antwerp, however, is the beauty of Rubens's religious art, which shows a perfect balance of worldly sensuality and spiritual longings. Although far more lavish than northern Dutch art, his *Descent from the Cross,* displayed in Antwerp's cathedral, is as profound as anything by Rembrandt. (More of Rubens's ecclesiastical works

A bedroom in René Magritte's apartment, now a museum, in Brussels.

are on view in the town of Ghent, in the St. Bavo Cathedral. The masterpiece, *The Conversion of St. Bavo*, hangs in a chapel there.)

As soon as you enter Brussels, to the south, you know you are in the French half of Belgium. Officially the city is bilingual; street signs are in French and Dutch. Brussels has a history that is at least as grand as Antwerp's. Tourists come to gawk at the gilded magnificence of the Grand Place, with its 15th-century town hall and, among other splendors, the 17th-century Zwaan Huis, formerly a prison and a court-house, and the place where Karl Marx wrote the Communist Manifesto. The Brussels of the 19th century was stranger and more opulent—the capital of a small, newly independent nation that was trying to impress or even one-up its neighbors.

In a southern suburb of Brussels, you'll find René Magritte's house, now a museum. Magritte lived modestly with his wife in a small apartment, where he also did his painting. His name is still on the door. Rather than trying to outdo the French Surrealists, the artist turned his bland, suburban style into the stuff of his own artistic reveries. ✦

For The Guide, see page 271.

A cobblestoned street in Antwerp, left. Below, top to bottom: An outline of a necklace at Katz Jewellers; an antique bracelet with rose-cut stones at Adelin.

THE PERFECT FIT

Shopping for Diamonds in Antwerp

SOME PEOPLE'S IDEA OF A DREAM TRIP is lying on the beach. For others nothing beats wandering around a drizzly Northern European city, peering into glittering shop windows. The latter may want to head to Antwerp, which has the vastest selection of diamonds in the world (some at savings of between 30 and 70 percent).

One of the best places to begin is Diamond House, in the jewelry district. Call proprietor Rob van Beurden a week before your arrival to explain what you want. Looking for a three-carat stone? He likely has a dozen exquisite examples.

To observe cutters and setters in action, visit Diamondland, an exhibit space and salesroom where the public can watch through windowed booths—not unlike watching the animals at the famous Art Nouveau zoo a few blocks away. Or stop in at one of the city's most reputable sources, Katz Jewellers, whose diamond-district digs have a marble fireplace and a chandelier.

For vintage diamonds, stop by antique-jewelry shop Adelin. Here, it's not about mere size, sparkle, or color—it's about the poetry of the setting and the history behind each facet, which can make a piece sing. ✦

For The Guide, see page 272.

DUTCH DESIGN

The Look of Amsterdam Today

IN THE LEGENDARILY TOLERANT Dutch capital, locals' innate talent for taking the everyday and making it supercool has landed the city squarely in the

Balsam wood lamps at WonderWood, a boutique in Amsterdam.

Housewares emporium Pol's Potten, in Amsterdam, right. Below: Gilt-dipped porcelain by Studio Job. Opposite: A view of the Amstel River.

global design spotlight.

Among cognoscenti, the names of Dutch designers have taken on near-totemic status: Hella Jongerius, Marcel Wanders, Jurgen Bey, Piet Hein Eek, Tejo Remy. They have all contributed so much to Holland's current stature that it is a little startling to recall that most were unknown before the debut, at the 1993 Milan Furniture Fair, of a Dutch collective called Droog.

For that first show, Droog's founders, Renny Ramakers and Gijs Bakker, cracked the lacquered surface of the design world with a bunch of materially humble and intellectually sophisticated objects that were unlike anything else. A dresser was made from secondhand drawers jumbled atop one another and loosely held with a belt. A bookcase was formed of compressed paper. A chair was shaped from bundled rags lashed with industrial packing straps.

These same objects, of course, now turn up everywhere— at New York shops like Moss, at high-end auctions held by Phillips de Pury, and even at Design '05 in Miami, where a New York dealer sold as a rarefied object Remy's aforementioned chest of drawers, charging roughly what a BMW might cost. That the dresser is still in production at

Droog—whose Amsterdam headquarters is a simple attic space—might be reason enough to get on a plane.

A visitor to shops like Pol's Potten or the Frozen Fountain, with their deftly edited selection of furniture and accessories, can hardly fail to note the embrace of the country's layered history. There are humorous rugs by Claudy Jongstra, felted from the wool of sheep she raises herself. And there's the porcelain service Bey recently produced for venerable manufacturer Royal Tichelaar Makkum (the oldest company in the Netherlands, founded in 1594). It's made with clay mined from prehistoric Friesian deposits, using molds and relief techniques that date back to the 17th century.

Some of the most interesting work at the city's design galleries incorporates the historic and the contemporary. At WonderWood, dealer Wiet Hekking displays 20th-century objects alongside pieces by Droog alumni and newcomers like Karel de Boer. Also present is work by Studio Job, a firm whose principal, Job Smeets, ranks among the Dutch design world's current stars. He uses craft forms like marquetry—an inlaid-wood technique—that are as old as the guilds. ✦

For The Guide, see page 272.

SWEDE TASTE

Stockholm's Food Scene

A deconstructed dessert at Lux, in Stockholm, left. Below: Gondolen, the tramcar bar. Opposite: The dining room at Riche.

DINERS WHO COME TO THE SWEDISH capital expecting only smorgasbords are in for a surprise. Stockholm's innovative chefs are making unabashedly artful food.

At the Michelin-starred Lux, Henrik Norström and Peter Johansson riff on familiar dishes with unlikely twists, like chicken soup that combines a creamy foam of cauliflower and truffle oil with poached quail eggs. The mood inside the 1907 red-brick building is soothing, with lamps that resemble orbs of spider's silk.

Set in a redesigned 1890's mansion, Riche is a labyrinth of rooms. The menu is filled with international all-star classics such as steak tartare, *frisée aux lardons*, and schnitzel. The adjoining lounge, Lilla Baren, hosts cutting-edge DJ's and occasional live shows.

Call it a day (or a night) with a drink and a skyline view in the Södermalm neighborhood at the tramcar-in-the-sky Gondolen. Erik Lallerstedt, a puckish chef with two other popular spots, Bakficka and Vinbar, serves dishes with a Swedish spin, including grilled halibut with lime beurre blanc and new potatoes. Also a draw: Swedish *snaps* (bitter and herbal schnapps), aquavit, and the local lagers Falcon and Pripps.

The next morning, head to Riddarbageriet, a small bakery with room for only six or eight people. It's worth the wait for perfect Swedish breakfast carbs: cardamom-and-cinnamon bread and pastries made with fresh lingonberries. ✚

For The Guide, see page 272.

Apropos Cöln, a fashionable boutique in Cologne, Germany, below and right. Opposite: Designer Fenja Ludwig at Atelier Ludvik.

COSMOPOLITAN COLOGNE

Germany's New Modern Center

THE ANCIENT ROMAN CITY OF COLOGNE HAS EMERGED as a star in western Germany, thanks to its rich art scene and a growing community of young international designers who have opened shops here. The city's compact, pedestrian-friendly layout makes exploring a breeze.

The Friesen district teems with design studios that double as storefronts, all run by rising talent. You're likely to find Fenja Ludwig piecing together funky feminine clothes in her workshop, Atelier Ludvik. Nearby, Lebanese-born Perla Zayek's namesake boutique showcases her silk evening dresses. The airy Walter König bookstore is a one-stop destination for photography junkies. And fashionistas pick up Jil Sander, Dolce & Gabbana, and Prada at Apropos Cöln, where expats can also stock up on English-language magazines. ✚

For The Guide, see page 272.

WHERE TO STAY

Hopper St. Antonius
Request a room at this high-design hotel with a view of Cologne's Gothic cathedral.

Hotel Santo An oasis of feng shui—all orchids and open spaces.

Hotel im Wasserturm
A former 19th-century brick water tower with sun-drenched rooms.

LEIPZIG ON VIEW

Europe's Next Art Capital

BEFORE THE WAR, THIS STATELY SAXON CITY in eastern Germany was a hub of culture and commerce. Thanks to a group of acclaimed neorealist painters and photographers, and influential dealers, Leipzig is becoming Europe's new center for art. During big opening weekends, flashy convertibles from Italy and the Czech Republic can be seen across town, and collectors from as far away as Korea and the United States arrive at Leipzig-Halle Airport in private jets.

Leipzig's Spinnerei complex, a former mill converted to artists' studios, top left. Clockwise from top right: At Galerie Eigen + Art; Café Neubau; Jean-Jacques Lebel's *Pur Porc, Lénine* at the Museum der Bildenden Künste. Opposite: An installation at the museum.

Housed in turn-of-the-19th-century brick cotton mills, the vast Spinnerei complex is the center of the scene. It currently contains nine commercial galleries; two nonprofit spaces; a venue for experimental installations; and roughly 80 studios. Works by art-world superstars like Neo Rauch can be found at Galerie Eigen + Art, an influential space founded by Gerd Harry Lybke, who moved his original 1983 gallery to Spinnerei in April 2004. Once Lybke—the undisputed leader of the local community—arrived, other gallerists followed. Spinnerei's latest addition is a satellite of the Williamsburg, Brooklyn–based Pierogi gallery.

Leipzig was spared the devastation suffered by neighboring Dresden during the war, and much of the city's gilded Baroque architecture survives, alongside Communist-era buildings. The Museum der Bildenden Künste sits squarely between relics of two architectural periods: the empty hulks of dour housing blocks and the Katharinenstrasse's neat file of sherbet-hued Baroque houses. The building doesn't look like much from the outside: a plain box with parts of its skin cut away to reveal two-story

Man with Mask by Wolfgang Mattheuer, at the Museum der Bildenden Künste, top left. Clockwise from top right: Leipzig's cobblestoned streets; Erró's *Good-bye Vietnam* at the Museum der Bildenden Künste; exhibition night at the Leipzig Academy.

T+L Tip

For an extensive list of exhibitions on view throughout the city, check out the Web site rundgang-kunst.de.

glass atriums around the perimeter. But inside, double-height galleries filled with daylight and finished in blond wood showcase contemporary work from Leipzig School artists alongside 18th- and 19th-century canvases and sculptures by Max Klinger and Caspar David Friedrich.

Another prominent venue in town is Galerie für Zeitgenössiche Kunst (Gallery for Contemporary Art), or GfZK, where one wing features works that explore post-socialist life, created by Leipzig artists and colleagues from other former Soviet Bloc regions. As GfZK curator Ilina Koralova puts it, in every sense, "Leipzig is back." +

For The Guide, see page 272.

MOZART'S MAGIC

Experience Two Centuries of Musical Tradition in Salzburg and Vienna

ALTHOUGH HE LIVED ONLY 35 YEARS (1756–1791), Mozart wrote more than 600 musical works spanning an array of genres. The two great Austrian cities most associated with him—Vienna and Salzburg—reveal an evolving Austria with much more in the Mozart department than powdered wigs.

In old Vienna people lived an average of 47 to a building, according to a chronicle of 1786. You can visit one

A view of Salzburg, Austria.

Mozart's birthplace, in Salzburg, left. Above: The Mozart memorial, in Vienna. Opposite: The ceiling of the 1735 National Library, in Vienna, where Mozart once gave concerts.

of Mozart's former apartments, which has been restored and comprises part of a museum called Mozarthaus Vienna.

Not far from St. Stephen's Cathedral, the museum is the only surviving Mozart residence in the capital; he lived there from 1784 to 1787, during which time he wrote *The Marriage of Figaro*. In one small room, possibly where Mozart composed his music, an extraordinary stucco detail from the period survives. The upper floors of the house contain displays about the operas, and there's a small performance space that's been carved out of part of the basement.

The Theater an der Wien, the city's newest opera venue, was reconstructed in 2006 as part of the composer's 250th-birthday celebration. Originally built in 1801, it is horseshoe-shaped and well-proportioned, accommodating an audience of only 1,000—a wonderful place to take in new stagings of Mozart operas, as well as co-productions with other European theaters, mounted by leading directors.

Mozart was born in Salzburg, and he was famously impatient to escape the city, so it is ironic that the place he disdained now lays claim to one of the world's most distinguished opera festivals. Begun in 1920, the annual six-week-long summer Salzburger Festspiele provides a showcase for Austrian culture and Mozart in particular. As the festival has increased in international fame, various parts of the festival's current theatrical complex have been updated. An expansion of the House for Mozart, a 1925 theater, provided the structure with a new intimacy as well as improved acoustics and sight lines.

It is amazing to see that more than 250 years after the composer's birth, Austria still resonates with Mozart's music and the vibrant new work it inspires. ✦

For The Guide, see page 273.

Sardines and caramelized red peppers with *bagna cauda* gelato, at LaLibera, left. Below: A view of Castiglione Falletto, in Piedmont. Opposite: Flavia Boffa, owner of Osteria LaLibera in Alba, Italy, with chef Marco Forneris.

DISHES OF PIEDMONT

A Culinary Journey in Northern Italy

FOR DEDICATED GASTRONOMES, a trip to Piedmont, south of Turin, is the Holy Grail, with its promise of long lunches and bold red wines. In many ways, Piedmont is Italy's gastronomic capital, thanks to the frenzy that surrounds white-truffle season each fall. But it is also here, amid the wine-making towns scattered through the hills of Asti and Alba, that the grapes for austere, elegant Barolos and Barbarescos as well as fizzy, bubble-gum-fresh Moscatos have been cultivated for centuries. It is here, too, that you find Cherasco, a hilltop town with a reputation for having the tastiest snails in the world, and Bra, the seat of Slow Food, the international movement of people dedicated to preserving the tradition of handmade, artisanal cuisine.

On Saturdays, the open-air market in Alba—the city that serves as the urban center for the surrounding towns of the Langhe region—teems with old-timers stuffing their mesh shopping bags with opal-hued baby artichokes, the local ricotta variation called Seirass, and black Livornese hens. In October, the truffles for which the town is most famous begin appearing. Down one of the side streets leading away from the market center is La Bottega del Vicoletto, a contemporary deli that sells sweet roasted peppers, slippery and cold and perfect on a hot morning. Buy ingredients for brunch there and then enjoy a picnic in the ample shade

found in the Piazza Savona.

Serious food lovers congregate at Osteria LaLibera, a quiet place in the sleepiest corner of the bustling southern end of Alba. The kitchen—so small that a sous-chef peels potatoes in an open courtyard behind the restaurant—doesn't miss a beat: grilled sardines come on caramelized Piedmontese peppers, with a scoop of *bagna cauda* gelato; and veal fillet, perfectly medium-rare, is served with a scattering of capers and chopped tomatoes on top.

A number of smaller towns deserve a visit. In Castelmagno, the namesake cheese that Slow Food founder Carlo Petrini has called "the flavor of the future" can be found in a few houses built into the mountain (look for hand-lettered FORMAGGI signs along the road). The farmers you encounter are likely to give enthusiastic tours of their cheese-making rooms and dark, damp aging caves before selling you their cheese. Fresh from the source, it has an almost chalky texture, and a pleasant tartness balanced by nutty notes.

Moving northeast, picturesque Cherasco is home to the Istituto Internazionale di Elicicoltura, a research facility dedicated to the farming of snails. Head to Osteria de la Rosa Rossa, where reservations are notoriously hard to get, both because of the restaurant's size—12 tables—and its reputation as the real deal in a tourist town.

The courtyard at Marchesi Alfieri castle and winery in Asti, above. Right: *Agnolotti del plin*, at LaLibera in Alba. Opposite, from left: Seasonal produce at Alba's morning market; sipping Barolo at Osteria de la Rosa, in Cherasco.

And in the stucco settlement of Rocchetta Tanaro, you'll find the trattoria I Bologna. From the cheese course of sheep's-milk Robiola, which has the texture of a soufflé, to the sparkly dessert wine Brachetto d'Acqui, which erupts with the scent of wild roses, the meal is exactly the kind of taste experience one should seek in Piedmont: focused and uncluttered—even simple—yet entirely new and exceptional. The *agnolotti del plin*, in particular, are a kind of angel-food entrée—each one a postage stamp's worth of minced pork, veal, cheese, and summer truffles stuffed into a paper-thin, tender egg pocket.

No visitor should leave without sampling what Piedmont's wine country has to offer. The area is unlike Napa. There are very few places that welcome impromptu tours, and the ones that do generally don't make wines you'd go out of your way to drink. Thankfully, most towns feature *enotecche regionale*, shops that carry many, if not all, the vintages from a particular region. In Barolo, the Enoteca Regionale del Barolo consists of a vaulted brick chamber in a turreted castle, where sommeliers in long black aprons pour from about 60 different vintages. Alternately, you could visit the Marchesi Alfieri, a spacious, tastefully appointed farmhouse-turned-hotel with outstanding views, on the grounds of a winery famed for its Barbera d'Asti. ✤

For The Guide, see page 273.

ITALIAN IDYLL

Scenic Day-Trip Drives Through Le Marche

LE MARCHE IS A LESSER-KNOWN PART OF ITALY, with a 111-mile-long coastline—a protruding left hip into the Adriatic Sea—and stretches of unspoiled countryside extending into Umbria. The best way to see Le Marche is by car. For speed, take the A14, which connects the entire region; but for pleasure, drive the *strade statali*, a slower route through beautiful landscapes. You can go practically anywhere in the area, taking the coastal highway, and be back where you started by nightfall.

Le Marche's treasures are scattered all over the area's towns. Ancona is a good place to base yourself, if only because it's easy to rent a car there, and it's home to the Hotel Emilia, which has spare interiors punctuated by stylish Achille Castiglioni lighting. The hotel provides a shuttle to and from its pebbled beach. In Ancona, ascend the highest hill overlooking the Adriatic to the medieval Cathedral of San Ciriaco. Inside, there is a 16th-century painting of the Virgin, who is said to protect travelers from storms at sea.

A winding road leads north to Senigallia's coast, where raked sands are ornamented by clusters of umbrellas and deck chairs. People come from all over Europe to places like Senigallia, with its medieval center and a few hundred cafes and *bagni*, which are packed from late morning until sunset. At the fish restaurant Uliassi, run by chef Mauro Uliassi and his sister, Catia, take a spot on the terrace and look out onto the limitless gray-green sea. The restaurant's *fritto*—with tiny tender octopus, and sticks of zucchini and eggplant—combines the best

Honey-colored hills near Urbino, typical of Le Marche.

aspects of tempura and Italian frying.

Driving south along the coast, at Monte San Giusto, travelers can see Lorenzo Lotto's Crucifixion, the altarpiece in the tiny church of Santa Maria in Telusiano. Mary, wrapped in a veil, is collapsing to the ground.

The region's hilltops have also inspired poets. Recanati, for instance, is a pilgrimage site for writers. Its glory is the 19th-century poet Giacomo Leopardi, who immortalized a hill in "The Infinite," Italy's most celebrated sonnet. Visit Leopardi's extraordinary library, assembled by his father, Count Monaldo. In the historic center of town, you can also see Lotto's Annunciation at the Colloredo-Mels museum. The artist, who was born in Venice around 1480, lived in Le Marche early in his career, and moved back there toward the end of his life.

Even Urbino, with its masterpieces of Renaissance architecture, would be hard to imagine without the surrounding hills, visible from every balcony of the Palazzo Ducale. Tour the arched spaces of the stables, the kitchens, and the duke's bathing chamber. His study, the Studiolo del Duca, is a cubicle paneled with intricately inlaid wood. Like most sites in Le Marche, it is a hidden treasure that anyone can see. ✦

For The Guide, see page 273.

Catia Uliassi at her Uliassi restaurant, in Senigallia, top right. Right: A 1531 Crucifixion-scene altarpiece by Lorenzo Lotto, at the Church of Santa Maria in Telusiano. Opposite: The courtyard of the Palazzo Ducale.

PLVRIES · DEPVGNAVIT · SEXIES · S

HIDDEN ROME

Unexplored Neighborhoods in the Italian Capital

Along Piazza Vittorio, in Rome's Esquilino
district, left. Above: Trattoria Monti.
Opposite: A car decorated for a wedding
in Rome's Testaccio neighborhood.

IN ITALY, A CERTAIN NUMBNESS and fatigue can accompany
seeing one more Caravaggio swaddled in a church's faint light,
one more imperial aqueduct commanding you to stand back
and admire it. Rome can leave you thinking that beauty should
have its limits, that visual poverty yields unexpected riches.
The neighborhoods Esquilino and Testaccio are a case in point.

Esquilino and Testaccio will never blister your camera
finger; but these precincts—the first an immigrant enclave,
the second a working-class wonderland—will make you ap-
preciate contemporary Rome at its most interesting, at its most
global, at its most youthful, and, when it comes to the restaurants, at its most satisfying.

The past few years have seen an influx of energy in Esquilino, once the most tired of Rome's seven hills. Piazza Vittorio—
Esquilino's enormous green heart, with endless salmon-hued
arcades—was laid out by the Turinese after Italy's unification

in the 1870's. Now, at the start of the
21st century, all that rational Northern
planning has given way to a melt-
ing pot that would make New York's
Lower East Side proud.

The church of Santa Bibiana is a
fitting representation of the neighborhood as a whole. It is squeezed in
between a tunnel and a smokestack,
fronted by tram tracks, and across from
an adult-video store. The façade was
the first architectural work of Baroque
wonder boy Bernini, and the interior is
a tiny jewel. The intimacy of the space
contrasts with the gilded overdrive
of Rome's more famous churches, and

A cardinal having lunch at Sora Rosa in Testaccio, right. Below: Cured meats at Volpetti, a deli in Testaccio.

the beatific Bibiana holding the palm leaf of martyrs fills the church with kindness and calm.

Just off the piazza is Trattoria Monti, known to many for its tall, dark waiters, the brothers Enrico and Daniele. There is no denying that very serious food (codfish carpaccio with red onions and truffles) is served within this intimate, barrel-vaulted space.

Located in the southern part of the central city, the neighborhood of Testaccio is all about animal attraction. The enormous *mattatoio*, the city's main slaughterhouse until it closed in 1975, was the center of economic life

for almost a century. The slaughterhouse is gone, but its spirit lives on in the Testaccio covered market, acknowledged by many to be the best in Rome. The neighborhood is also the home base for the real cucina romana, embracing the so-called fifth quarter—the leftover parts of the animal (tripe, nerves, Adam's apple)—along with Jewish and regional country favorites such as fried artichokes and anchovies. After dining in a leisurely fashion on a piece of intestine and a glass of affordable red, many people head to Monte Testaccio, a bizarre mountain built entirely out of discarded amphorae that is now home to Rome's most interesting dance clubs. The knowledgeable, chill crowd goes to Metaverso, a small white cave festooned with Keith Haring–type graphic art where reggae and electronica rule. There's something oddly inspiring about middle-class Italian boys in dreadlocks trying to do Jamaican dance-hall steps. ✚

For The Guide, see page 273.

SEMPRE NAPOLI

Italy's Most Vibrantly Authentic City

NAPLES IS ONE OF THE FEW CITIES LEFT IN EUROPE that retains the power to intoxicate: a grand port that operates as though the earth were yet a sphere of wonders with itself at the magnetic center. A novelist once noted that Naples induced a hallucinatory sense of looking through a veil of time, at things occurring just as they might have hundreds of years ago. Italians in other regions speak of Naples as though it were not part of modern Italy. That may be what lies behind its appeal.

The streets that slash through the Centro Storico and the lanes that ramp down sticky, cobbled hillsides were built in Roman times. There are still cameo carvers, coral workers, and the finest *stuccatores*, as well as candy makers at the Gay-Odin factory who turn out sweets called Tears of Love. Sitting

A view of Naples from the hilltop museum Certosa di San Martino.

NAPLES'S TOP SHOPS.

Sartoria Napoletana is the name of the tradition of male dandyism for which Naples is justly renowned. Milan remains the capital of Italian fashion, of course, but this is where you will find some of the country's finest tailors and men's shops.

Borrelli Justifiably famous—and expensive—men's wear.

Eddy Monetti Clothes typical of the Neapolitan style for him and her.

Magnifique Custom-made and ready-to-wear men's shirts and shoes.

Marinella The city's most revered source for ties.

Milord Clothing for hipper Neapolitan males.

Nino di Nicola Affordably priced and well-made suits and shirts.

at a restaurant along the waterfront—like Gusto & Gusto, where the staff wears crisply ironed orange aprons—you get the impression that you've wandered right into another era.

There's enough here to keep a visitor occupied for three lifetimes, as opposed to the three days guidebooks claim are sufficient—from the new Museo d'Arte Contemporanea Donna Regina (MADRE) to the opera house to the National Archaeological Museum, with its renowned Roman bust of the emperor Caracalla, vain and sexy, with his cruel gaze and deeply cleft chin. Or the strikingly fresh ancient mosaics in the baptistery of the Duomo. Or the Capodimonte museum, a huge palazzo with a kooky 1425 Assumption by Tommaso di Cristoforo Fini, where dozens of angels swarm like bats.

Few things build an appetite like a morning of Annuncia-

tions and Flagellations. From the hilltop where the Capodimonte is situated, hike back toward the city center to the
celebrated restaurant Europeo Mattozzi, owned for the past
century by the same family. From a table in front, you'll have a
view of the resident *pizzaiolo* flipping dough in the old-world
way. Most pizzas in Naples are prepared in more or less the
same sort of oven, at the same temperature (700 degrees), with
the same two-inch "lip," and using the same mozzarella and industrial tomato sauce. The ones here, however, have been
declared some of the best. The rest of the food at Europeo is
equally seductive, with huge globes of buffalo mozzarella,
antipasti of fried zucchini flowers, and *fragaglie*, tiny fish that are
deep-fried and startlingly good. ✛

For The Guide, see page 274.

**The Mattozzi family at their restaurant Europeo
Mattozzi, in Naples, above left. Above right:
The courtyard at Certosa di San Martino.
Opposite: Corso Umberto I in Centro Storico.**

At the Agatha
Ruiz de la
Prada shop in
L'Eixample.

GONE
SHOPPING

The Stylish Boutiques of Barcelona

Riding through Barcelona's Barri Gòtic neighborhood, above.

FROM THE MEDIEVAL BARRI GÒTIC to the white-hot El Born, Barcelona's shopping neighborhoods have made the city a way station on the international fashion trail, drawing hordes of pilgrims with fat Fendi purses and Marni coats.

In Barri Gòtic, there's the quintessential Barcelona espadrille store, La Manual Alpargatera, which is so crowded customers have to take a number. It's steeped in history (Salvador Dalí was a customer) but still claims unimpeachable street cred (Jean Paul Gaultier is a client). Nearby, Cereria Subirà is a centuries-old candle store in business since 1761, with tapers shaped like mountains, mushrooms, and Mickey Mouse.

To the north, the district of L'Eixample is renowned for its concentration of turn-of-the-20th-century Modernist architecture. Some of the city's finest shops line the boulevard Passeig de Gràcia. Custo Barcelona has an abundance of wildly printed tops; Agatha Ruiz de la Prada (no relation to Miuccia) also appeals to giddy spirits, with pieces such as polka-dot sweaters. At the the spectacularly designed Carolina Herrera store, ruffly dresses and city sneakers embellished with the CH logo are a big hit with the locals. (Carolina may be Venezuelan, but her daughter is married to the Spanish former bullfighter Miguel Báez.) Unlike Herrera, Adolfo Dominguez, whose busy boutique is a full-service

T+L Tip

Plan for long afternoon
siestas, since locals take
their four-hour lunch
breaks (typically from 12:30
to 4:30 p.m.) seriously.
And most stores are also
closed on Sunday.

Shoes at Barcelona's Agatha Ruiz de la Prada, above left. Above right: Inside Corium. Opposite: Contemporary furniture at Vinçon.

depot for upper-middle-class Barcelo-
nese, is an authentic native son, having
grown up in Galicia. His conservative
styles (office-ready trousers, pleated
skirts) are enlivened with bursts of
color. Corium, connected to the Omm
Hotel, has a shrewdly edited stock of
international designs. And if you find
yourself momentarily tired of clothes,
descend upon Vinçon, where lamps
appear to be inspired by everything
from life rafts to salt rocks.

Once known for its run-down
warehouses, El Born district is now a
bohemian hub. Stop by Agua del Carmen for dresses in nutty
corduroy, or Beatriz Furest for pale gray-green hunting bags.
The retail star of the neighborhood, though, is Lobby, which
sells outré clothes from hometown labels like Roca and Who.

The anchor of the Gràcia neighborhood is the Mercat de la
Llibertat, a covered food market where Barcelona's matrons still
do their grocery shopping in gabardine suits. The low-key quarter
is being gentrified by a number of innovative and offbeat
designers, but at La Cova del Col.leccionisme, a rigorously
curated ephemera shop, you'll see that the city's credentials as a
stylish metropolis are anything but new: vintage issues of a
1920's magazine called *La Doña Catalana* showcase breathtaking
Art Deco fashions on every page. ✦

For The Guide, see page 274.

The entrance to northern Spain's literary festival, in Gijón. Right: Comic-book artists on a train, en route to the festival.

PULP FICTION

A Literary Festival in the Small Town of Gijón

CALL IT A CELEBRATION OF PULP AND DARKNESS. Every summer for the past 18 years, Semana Negra ("Black Week"), a literary festival devoted to noirish, outsider literature, has drawn thousands to Gijón, a trim and stylish town of well-kept 19th-century houses in northern Spain. Honoring often-dismissed writers of mystery, thrillers, science fiction, and comic books from around the world, the festival is now one of the largest in Europe.

The brainchild of left-leaning Spanish thriller writer Paco Ignacio Taibo (who lives in Mexico), it's all pretty strange. During the festivities, the entrance to Gijón's fairgrounds is marked by an immense statue of a redhead in a sexy dress climbing up a tottering stack of books. Crowds wind their way through a carnival landscape laced with book stands and makeshift monuments commemorating great mystery and science-fiction writers. Brilliantly costumed Peruvian girls sell belts. Senegalese men in their twenties hawk eyeglass cases. Hundreds of vendors grill chorizo and man immense vats of boiling octopus.

The intellectual center of Semana Negra is a huge tent where lectures, readings, and signings take place. Many of these events, in true Spanish fashion, begin near midnight.

"To me," says festival founder Taibo, "there is no contradiction between great fun and great books." +

For The Guide, see page 274.

BASQUE GLORY

Contemporary Design Comes to a Quiet Spanish Hamlet

THE TOWN OF ELCIEGO, population 900, is cradled in the Basque country of northern Spain. The village is conservative, unsentimental, immaculate, and timeless, with a ravishing cathedral and a proud dourness that is rather charming. In observance of

A view of Elciego village from the Hotel Marqués de Riscal's breakfast terrace.

T+L Tip

Rioja wine–related festivals occur in and around Elciego in June and September; for more information, go to elciego.es.

The Hotel Marqués de Riscal's mirror-steel exterior in Elciego, Spain, above. Left: The Cathedral, the hotel's wine cellar.

an old Basque custom, sunflowers hang over thresholds to keep out the wrong kind of spirits.

The residents here are still working out their feelings about the biggest thing to ever hit their village: the Hotel Marqués de Riscal, beribboned in luscious titanium and designed by superstar architect Frank Gehry. In 2006, the hotel raised its tousled head among the Rioja vines of the 148-year-old Herederos del Marqués de Riscal winery.

Despite the new resident, Elciego remains unspoiled by tourists. Dinner for two at La Cueva, which serves oversize portions of pork-studded lentils in vaulted rooms, can still be had for $25. Travelers can step off the Main Square and into Vinoteca La Ermita to buy Idiazabal cheese and wines from local producers, such as Viña Salceda and Murúa. Stop by the Elciego tourism office for tickets to see the 16th-century Iglesia de San Andrés, which has both Gothic and Renaissance characteristics. Then it's back to the curved-steel petals of the hotel, which seems like a dramatic extension of the surrounding landscape—transforming Elciego, but also transformed by it. ✦

For The Guide, see page 274.

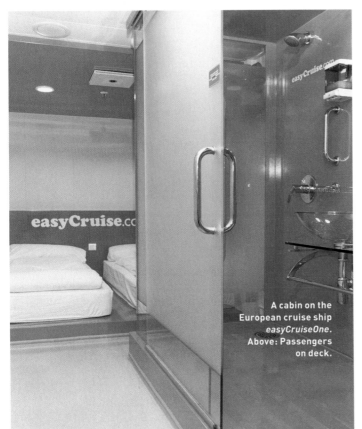

A cabin on the European cruise ship *easyCruiseOne*. Above: Passengers on deck.

SHIP SHAPE

Take an Affordable Cruise in Europe

SUSPEND YOUR DISBELIEF, AND IMAGINE this: a cruise through Europe that costs only about $200 for a three-night stay. Launched by easyGroup (known in Europe for its affordable airline and hotels), the no-frills *easyCruiseOne* island-hops throughout Greece. (There's also a sister ship *easyCruiseTwo*, which plies the waters around Holland and Belgium.)

On departures from May through October, you can experience the blue-green waters of the Aegean Sea, stopping at a different Cycladic island each day. There's a selection of itineraries, ranging from two nights to seven. Mykonos, Naxos, Poros: the ports sound more like those of a chartered yacht, not a bright orange ship full of budget travelers. On land, passengers take part in daytime beach parties or dine at hilltop tavernas.

The view from the ship—when the air is fresh and the Aegean is a universe of glitters—is equally alluring. The cabins are not spacious, but they have a cockpit aesthetic. And once you're in one of the Jacuzzis by the open-air cocktail bar, you'll experience another kind of beauty. There you are, anchored on the wine-dark sea with a drink, watching people have similar experiences in the hot tubs of yachts that couldn't have left much change from $5 million, while you're paying mere pennies. ✦

For The Guide, see page 274.

T+L Tip

The Turkish port of Çesme is only 45 minutes by ferry from Chios. It is a good day trip (no visa is required). Wander the bustling streets and market stalls, where you'll find odd bits of things like spices, sweets, and motorcycle jackets.

QUIET ISLE
Escape to Chios in Greece

JUST OFF TURKEY'S WEST COAST, the island of Chios has a complicated history, not all of it pretty. Greece's war of independence in the 1820's, which ended 400 years of Turkish rule, was a bloody affair. It's hard to imagine the turmoil today: beyond the port of Kambos, pear trees give way to orange groves and cypresses. On a distant hill, a monastery is visible. Chios is at its grandest at the Argentikon hotel, a restored 16th-century estate that sprawls behind a stone wall along a Kambos back road.

In the square at Pyrgi, locals sip *visináda*, a wild-cherry drink, at cafés surrounded by geometric-patterned houses. Nearby is the medieval city of Mesta, its Old Town a maze of stone buildings and shady squares.

At the southern tip of the island is Emboriós, with its beach of charcoal-colored lava pebbles. Dine under olive trees at O Kambos taverna, on the ground floor of an old house.

Don't leave without taking the steep 45-minute drive uphill to Anavatos. The view alone, of the Aegean Sea and Turkey beyond, is well worth the trip. ✛

For The Guide, see page 274.

A fishing boat at Emboriós, on the Greek island of Chios. Opposite, from left: the port's black-pebble beach; a building in Pyrgi.

ΚΩΣΤΑΝΤΗΣ
Λ.Χ. 1547

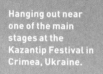

Hanging out near
one of the main
stages at the
Kazantip Festival in
Crimea, Ukraine.

EASTERN
EUROPE

MOUNTAIN MAJESTY

Roaming Through Bulgaria's Magnificent Rila Range

A shepherd in Govedartsi, in the Rila Mountains of southwestern Bulgaria, left. Below: Signs to Seven Lakes. Opposite: The Rila Monastery.

THE POCKET-SIZE RILA MOUNTAINS form the southwestern boundary of the Bulgarian heartland, their foothills rising from fields just an hour south of Sofia, the nation's capital. At Musala peak, the highest point in the Balkans, the range's sharp granite pinnacles assert an ancient ruggedness before falling off to the south, toward the drier areas along the Greek border.

Rila National Park, nearly the size of Yosemite, has alpine meadows and ancient evergreen stands surrounded by monastery land, Ministry of Forests and Agriculture acreage, and pastures belonging to villages and towns. This is long-forgotten primeval Europe, a place to find unchanged examples of Bulgarian culture.

The park is a choice spot for hiking, cycling, communing with shepherds, and visiting serene monasteries. The adventurous can bike down steep paths into wooded gorges, but many of the villages and chalets in the mountains are also accessible to those less inclined to physical exertion. Rustic stone inns have outdoor areas for a pre-hike snack of espresso and *banitsa*, a local pastry of phyllo-wrapped leeks and feta-like cheese.

In the hamlet of Govedartsi, a breakfast of sheep's-milk yogurt topped with wild honey and blueberries at the family-run House Djambazki tastes of the neighboring pastures. Served in a

The Rila Monastery, where visitors can stay in converted monks' cells, right. The road leading to the monastery, below.

stone-and-wood gazebo behind the inn, it's the perfect fortification for an afternoon climb through the pine-cloaked hillsides along the nearby Iskar River to the fields above, where shepherds tend their flocks.

Besides beauty, these mountains have history: the Bulgarian Orthodox Saint Ivan Rilski fled the secular world in 927 for a drafty cave deep in the beech forests. Pilgrims still attempt to pass through the cave's narrow opening; those who are able to make it are said to be free of sin. An easy hike from the cave, the Rila Monastery, with domes that sit like ripe figs atop a fanciful mille-feuille, is an important seat of the Bulgarian Orthodox Church and the most visited place in the nation. It has been in its present location since 1335. As dictated by the region's millennia-old tradition of hospitality, guests can stay at the monastery in converted (and surprisingly comfortable) monks' cells. In the morning, a monk's rhythmic tapping on a carved plank signals the beginning of the dawn service, and throughout the day, sacred fountains gurgle along the cloisters.

On the other side of the toothed ridge that towers above the monastery, through an alpine pass, are the Seven Lakes. It's a tough day's hike from the south, but well worth it: these vitreous jewels lie amid scree, where winter's snow lingers even in August. ✦

For The Guide, see page 275.

RETURN TO MONTENEGRO

A Comeback on the Adriatic Coast

ALTHOUGH THE WORLD HAS DISCOVERED CROATIA and its idyllic shores, neighboring Montenegro, a land of untouched white sands and time-capsule medieval villages, is still a well-kept secret. It wasn't always this way: the country once drew such Hollywood luminaries as Sophia Loren and Richard Burton to its 75-mile Adriatic coast. But the Iron Curtain and conflicts following the breakup of Yugoslavia kept many visitors at bay.

Happily, foreign tourism is on the rise. Jat Airways launched a direct flight from London, and a new tunnel takes drivers from the sleepy capital of Podgorica through the mountains directly to the coast. Butterfield & Robinson recently added Montenegro to a yacht-based trip in the area, and Amanresorts plans to restore Sveti Stefan—a 15th-century village of cobblestoned streets running along crescent-shaped beaches. At a growing list of top restaurants, small-batch wines are paired with freshly caught mussels and lobster. Plan a trip soon—before this Riviera is on everyone's radar. ✛

For The Guide, see page 275.

The coastal village of Perast, northeast of Herceg-Novi, in Montenegro.

GRAPE ESCAPE

The Heirloom Wines of Hungary

A vineyard on the Szeremley Estate, in western Hungary's Badacsony region, above. Right: Béla Fölfödi, Szeremley's winemaker, holding a traditional tasting pipette. Opposite: Szeremley's 200-year-old wine cellar.

ONCE UPON A TIME, HUNGARY'S WINES were the envy of the world. But like Spain and South Africa, Hungary was marginalized by politics during the second half of the 20th century, and its wine industry—along with much of the rest of the country—emerged from the shadows after the fall of European Communism in 1989 with plenty of catching up to do.

Local wineries have come quite a distance, but the bottles worth trying are produced by people staying true to their traditional roots. Quirky, temperamental, and white, Hungary's heirloom grapes are unlike any other in the world. Referred to as Hungaricum, the grapes are grown most successfully on the northern shore of Lake Balaton, a two-hour drive from Budapest, in the western part of the country. The lake is among the largest and shallowest in Europe, a cigar-shaped expanse that extends nearly 50 miles, southwest to northeast, across the Pannonian plain.

The wine-growing area remains a study in green. Driving in from the capital, the streets are lined with flower gardens and the traditional squat cottages of the region, with roofs of densely packed straw. The hotels tend to be small, family-run establishments.

Balaton wine is the equivalent of comfort food to many Hungarians—one reason it continues to thrive domestically even as the wider world's viticultural bounty floods the country.

Harvesting Pinot Gris grapes near Lake Balaton, right. Above: A traditional house in Somló, north of the lake. Opposite: The Wine Museum at Hotel Bacchus, in Keszhely, on the lake's northern shore.

Another reason is Hungary's cuisine, generally rich and spiced with paprika, which Balaton's wines cut right through, refreshing the mouth with their bright acidity, but also adding a complexity that emanates from the mineral-rich soil. At the Hotel Bacchus in Keszhely, which features some of the best food in the region, Balaton wines pair perfectly with the heaviness of liver dumplings and red cabbage.

Prominent local vintner Mihály Figula's decade-old winery was built on the site of a far older one, where vines have been cultivated continually for 2,000 years. He grows 12 varieties, and ships wine to nine countries. Figula's Riesling, Sauvignon Blanc, and Pinot Gris—reminiscent of a good Chablis—are terrific, but they're also familiar. His most interesting varietal is Zenit. It's a hybrid of two Hungaricum grapes and is slightly sweet, with a flavor of lychee nuts.

Five miles down a road edged by birch trees, the hillside Szeremley Estate, in Badacsonytomaj, produces more wines made from the elusive Hungaricum: Budai Zöld, light-hued, with notes of citrus, has a lilting elegance; darker Bakator has a gummy taste, almost like Riesling, yet utterly distinct; and Kéknyelü is the real revelation. At the winery's restaurant, a 1996 bottle is well matched with a meal of sliced tongue, white perch with a

5 BOTTLES TO BUY IN THE U.S.

Szeremley Muscat Ottonel Badacsony 2004
Perfumed and floral, with residual sweetness offset by acidity ($10).

Tibor Gál Egri Bikavér 2002
Traditional red from the Carpathians that fills the mouth with tannins and deep, old-world flavor ($16).

Weninger Spern Steiner Kékfrankos Selection Sopron 2003
A single-vineyard, single-grape wine from mineral-rich soil near Austria ($45).

Bock Jozsef Bock Cuvee Barrique Villány 1999
Spicy Cabernet Sauvignon–based blend from Hungary's southern border; it has one foot in Central Europe, the other in Bordeaux ($50).

Disznókö Tokaji Aszú 6 Puttonyos 2000
Gorgeous example of Hungary's Wine of Kings. Super-sweet yet refreshing, with pear, peach, and caramel flavors that will drink well for decades ($69).

Hungarian ratatouille, and a fillet of intensely flavored beef. A final treat: late-harvest Zeus—thick, honeyed, and nuanced.

Artisanal vintners like István Kiss are trying to preserve the country's more obscure varieties. Kiss is something of an underground legend in Hungarian wine circles. Everyone seems to know his name, but almost nobody has tasted his wines, which are bottled under the label Szent-György Pince. Philosophically opposed to wine's worldwide-distribution system, he sells only at local festivals and to friends and visitors of the winery, just as his predecessors might have done a century ago. But what wines! A transcendent Juhfark, bold and peppery; a Budai Zöld with the bite of a Granny Smith apple; a sharply acidic Furmint—wines that tell you that you could be nowhere else. ✦

For The Guide, see page 275.

Revelers take a break at the Kazantip Festival, on the Crimean Peninsula, in Ukraine, left. Below: A couple carrying yellow suitcases, a quirky tradition at the event. Opposite: Dancers in the Black Sea during the revelry.

UKRAINIAN BEACH PARTY

Dance All Day (and Night) at a Monthlong Festival in Crimea

AT THE KAZANTIP FESTIVAL IN CRIMEA, the barbarians aren't at the gate, they're on the beach. Revelers gather along Ukraine's Black Sea coast, about 375 miles north of Istanbul, for a four-to-six-week summer party that attracts tens of thousands of visitors each year.

DJ's from across Europe bring their records, and 10 stages are built right on the sand, surrounded by dancers gyrating and swaying. The music plays all night, and freedom is in the air. It's a carefree life here on the western edge of the Crimean Peninsula, near the hamlet of Popovka—a hedonistic corollary to the youthful demonstrations that swept Ukraine during 2004's Orange Revolution.

Kazantip is a dissident dance party, a subculture intended to transform a culture. Or perhaps: a party that reflects a transformation. The event has taken place each summer since 1993, and its quasi-political tenor is often explicitly silly—every year, the organizers publish a constitution which, for example, declares the party a "virtual republic" and bans tuxedos and bow ties.

Most of the partygoers—decked out in beads and sarongs or, sometimes, nothing—rent rooms in Popovka, and spend the afternoon sunning before showing up to dance around midnight. There's music playing almost 24 hours a day; the local roosters, their internal clocks confused by the nonstop activity, end up crowing all afternoon long. ✚

For The Guide, see page 275.

RIGA'S REVIVAL

Latvia's Capital Comes of Age

LIKE MANY CITIES IN EASTERN EUROPE that have a long history of foreign occupation and a more recent history of dramatic change, Riga is just getting to know itself. More so than most cities in the region, the capital of Latvia is in the midst of an identity-altering boom that gives it the impressionable mien of a rebellious teen.

Dozens of multinational businesses, giddy at low-cost Latvia's acceptance into the European Union in 2004, have opened offices in Riga, which is centrally located between the other two Baltic capitals—Tallinn, to the north, and Vilnius, to the south. Cue the tourism industry: European discount airlines have recently made Riga a direct-flight destination. And hoteliers have responded, too, putting up more than 30 properties in 2005 and 2006 alone. Among them is the Hotel Bergs, a restored brick 19th-century building topped with a sleek glass addition that befits the city's new scene.

The resulting influx of foreigners now finds Riga, the largest and most cosmopolitan city in the Baltics, alive with energy, ambition, and ideas.

Garage, an accessories shop in Riga's Bergs Bazaar, above. Left: A view of Riga. Opposite, from top: A local at Club Essential; a loft suite at the Hotel Bergs; Martins Ritins at his restaurant, Vincent's.

British chef Martins Ritins—whose Latvian parents fled the country during Communism—jump-started the restaurant scene in the 1990's. At Vincent's, Ritins has been building an international reputation for his innovative and dynamic dishes like local eel with celeriac and potato latkes (virtually every visiting statesman requests a meal cooked by him). Ritins also recently opened the only organic market in the city, launched his own TV show, and started a program to train aspiring Latvian cooks.

After years of neglect during Soviet times, the Bergs Bazaar area has been converted into an upscale shopping district, with several good restaurants and fashionable boutiques lining the Parisian-style arcade that runs between Marijas and Elizabetes Streets. One of the standouts is Garage. The gray-and-silver-toned housewares and accessories shop was designed by Riga's own Zaiga Gaile, the architect behind the Hotel Bergs.

And then there's the nightlife. Assuming you don't twist an ankle on the cobblestoned medieval streets, or consume too many shots of Black Balsam—the country's stiff signature cordial—it's possible to visit five or six places in a few hours. Due to the northerly location, summer days are pleasantly long, and things only really get going at 2 a.m. Some venues, like Club Essential, have so many levels and dance floors, they could pass muster in Los Angeles or Moscow. +

For The Guide, see page 276.

RUSSIA'S RIVIERA

The Black Sea Town of Sochi Gets a Makeover

A glimpse of the Black Sea, in the Russian resort town of Sochi, left. Below: One of the town's many casinos. Opposite: The lobby of Sochi's Grand Hotel Rodina.

THE TERM *RUSSIAN BEACH* HAS THE UNDENIABLE RING of an oxymoron. Russia is, after all, the land of reindeer, permafrost, and polar night—a place where people are occasionally killed by falling icicles. Tourists who come to this country do so for the girls, the weirdness, the flash, the spectacle, the party. Expatriates who work here do so for financial firms or for oil companies. But no one expects to get a tan.

Mere logic has never deterred the Russians from a building project, however. Sochi, for decades the Soviet Union's center for relaxation, is the latest recipient of a well-timed reinvention. Once the finest resort behind the Iron Curtain, it is set on a stretch of the easternmost side of the Black Sea, along the foothills of the western Caucasus Mountains; its dramatic black-stone beaches are swimmable from May through

the "velvet season," in late October.

Sochi, which means "juicy" in Russian, is at heart a flaming neon phoenix of a boardwalk town. On its main corner stands a giant mosaic of Lenin's head, perpetually wreathed in smoke billowing from carts of sizzling meat. Women wear high heels on the beach, and their proto-capitalist mates unironically chomp cigars as they stand in the shallows. The nightspots are a collective time machine set to 1980. Stalin had a dacha, or country house, here (now a kitschy hotel

A mosaic of Lenin, dating from the 1970's, right. Below: The Ordzhonikidze Sanatorium, one of Sochi's health spas.

and museum), and he encouraged the construction, starting in the 1920's, of sanatoriums—many of which are still in operation, running on fumes and faded glory. Until lately, that's been it.

Two years ago, in a successful bid to host the 2014 Winter Olympics, the Kremlin began funneling stratospheric amounts of cash into the development of Sochi, promising to spend billions to revitalize the entire region. The most notable manifestation of the new Sochi is the Grand Hotel Rodina, a $45 million resort that opened in July 2006.

Flaunting impeccable wild-Russian-luxury credentials, the Rodina is a stunning refurbishment of a Stalin-era villa, with characteristically soaring ceilings, acres of creamy marble, and manicured grounds leading down to a private beachfront.

It's still up in the air, however, whether the hotel is a pioneer on the frontier of Russian decadence or a lonely white elephant. Proof of the former: the Russian-language Kinotavr film festival, held in Sochi each June for the past 16 years, is gaining international attention; Putin himself has a resort-size personal dacha here, where he hosted an EU summit in May 2006; and a degree of star power comes from an elite tennis camp in the hills—the alma mater of, among others, Maria Sharapova. ✚

For The Guide, see page 276.

ARCHITECTURAL QUEST

Russia's Past Is Still Present in Novgorod

WALKING ALONG NOVGOROD'S SIDE streets, lined with linden trees and gracious prerevolutionary houses, is like going back in time to somewhere in the mid 19th century. An ancient settlement about 100 miles south of St. Petersburg, Novgorod was founded by a Viking in 862. By the 12th century, it had become one of the most influential city-states in Europe, and at its height Novgorod expanded north from St. Petersburg into what is now Finland.

The best way to experience the city is through a tour of its architecture. Despite being heavily bombed by the Nazis, Novgorod has a historic center that remains largely intact. During the

The outer walls of Novgorod's kremlin, constructed in the 15th century.

At the Vitoslavlitsy Museum
of Wooden Architecture, above. Right:
The Yurievsky Monastery. Far right:
A bridge over the Volkhov River.
Opposite: Frescoes in the 17th-century
Cathedral of Our Lady of the Sign.

city's golden age, ships sailed up the Volkhov River from Holland
and England to trade for amber and furs. A long wall of white
arches remains as a reminder of the old marketplace. Behind it
sits a cluster of onion-domed churches and the ruins of the palaces
of the former rulers known as the Yaroslavsky Court, which flourished from 1045 through the Middle Ages.

Inside Novgorod's kremlin—a 30-acre inner city surrounded
by a high brick wall—the main attraction is the Cathedral of St.
Sophia. In the dim, high-vaulted interior, babushkas bow before
the Znamensky Icon. Just outside the kremlin, the Fine Arts
Museum has an extraordinary collection of medieval icons, many
of them four or five feet tall. Across the river is the 17th-century
Cathedral of Our Lady of the Sign.

Even historic architecture from neighboring areas is now found
in Novgorod. Centuries-old log churches
from the surrounding villages have
been moved to the Vitoslavlitsy Museum
of Wooden Architecture. They are
masterpieces of wooden construction;
some have seamless dovetailed corners.

And then there's the Yurievsky
Monastery, its cupolas perched on
tall white towers. From the bridge
over the Volkhov River, they resemble
rocket ships ready to take off to
paradise amid a celestial launchpad
interrupting the landscape's flatness. ✚

For The Guide, see page 276.

A member of the
Hadza tribe, nomadic
hunter-gatherers who
live near Lake Eyasi,
in northern Tanzania.

AFRICA+ THE MIDDLE EAST

CUTTING-EDGE CAIRO Egypt's Electric Art Scene

MAAROUF, A NARROW STREET IN DOWNTOWN CAIRO, frequently echoes with the sound of mechanics reshaping steel. It is an unlikely setting in which to see fine art. Yet only one block south sits Townhouse, a white-walled gallery space with video installations and large-scale photographs. The juxtaposition of old and new is typical of Cairo: a century ago, this alley served as an entrance to a sprawling mansion. Now, it is home to the city's vibrant contemporary art scene.

For much of the 1990's, there were few independent galleries in Cairo, and they showed only traditional fine arts such as painting and sculpture. One of the established galleries, Mashrabia, exhibits a handful of contemporary artists like Ahmed Askalany, who makes anthropomorphic figures from woven palm leaves. But Townhouse, which opened in 1998—when a new generation was beginning to work in video, photography, and installation art—is now leading the pack showing emerging talents.

Amal Kenawy is one of Townhouse's most prominent artists. She mixes video projection and sculpture in pieces such as *The Journey*. Another, Moataz Nasr, used to work in paint and clay. Now he favors video. The shift has brought him critical acclaim—and success. A decade ago, Nasr shared $800 with a fellow painter to do a mural at the downtown restaurant Felfela; recently, his 2003 video installation *Tabla I* sold for about $40,000.

As interest in the scene grows, international curators have arrived in search of art that embodies Western notions of Middle Eastern identity. Some people have avoided the clichés. In her collages, Sabah Naim shows a side of Cairo that is neither modern nor traditional, but something in between: people making their way in the city, lost in thought. It's an idea that can seem radical in a country that will always be known for its antiquity. While the dynasties that built the pyramids have died out, the art of today has never been more alive. +

For The Guide, see page 276.

Artist Amal Kenawy, in her studio, connected to Townhouse, Cairo's top contemporary art gallery.

ALEXANDRIA RESURRECTED

New Sites in an Ancient Metropolis

FOR CENTURIES, ALEXANDRIA, EGYPT, was renowned for its library and the colossal Pharos, an iconic lighthouse that was listed by classical thinkers as one of the Seven Wonders of the World. But when Napoleon disembarked here in 1798, the city founded by Alexander the Great had been reduced to a humble fishing village. Earthquakes and fires had destroyed the celebrated wonders, and the city's animated cultural life had been leveled by the scourges of war.

During the past few years, Alexandria has reclaimed its role as a cultural beacon, thanks to its new library, the Bibliotheca Alexandrina, inaugurated in 2002, and the Alexandria National Museum, which opened in a restored Italianate villa a year later. A world-class hotel is joining these institutions: the 118-room Four Seasons San Stefano. Constructed on the site of a posh 1930's resort, it will be blessed with ocean breezes and sandy beaches and will have a European spa and three restaurants with views of the Mediterranean—an appropriate nod to the city's reawakened splendor. +

For The Guide, see page 276.

Alexandria's new Bibliotheca Alexandrina.

Avenue Mohammed V, one of Rabat's main thoroughfares, left. Below: A guest room at Dar Al Batoul hotel.

REFUGE IN RABAT

Morocco's Low-Key Capital

IT'S NO ACCIDENT THAT IN ARABIC, the name Rabat means "a retreat." Other Moroccan cities offer better-known diversions: the musky souks of Marrakesh; the dark warrens of Fez; the film-noir whiff of faded grace and veiled sin in Casablanca. But Rabat blends all this variety into a neat, well-proportioned package. Surprisingly, most travelers haven't yet caught on. This shortfall has its compensating advantages—namely, peace and quiet in a beautiful setting.

The walled Old Town is unexpectedly clean but authentically mazelike, with crowded bazaars, eerily empty alleyways, and a cliff-top castle by the ocean. Early evenings bring throngs of strollers onto Avenue Mohammed V, but their chatter never seems to rise above a murmur. In the palace quarter, silence emanates from the long, crenellated walls. Just beyond lie the gardens of Chellah, where storks and cats amble among Roman ruins and a medieval Muslim necropolis. This ensemble creates a primal tension that adds to the contemplative power of the place. At the end of the day, behind a studded wooden door, the Dar Al Batoul hotel awaits. It's a blend of simple comfort and high Moroccan style, all dappled shadow and bold color. +

For The Guide, see page 277.

INTO AFRICA

Tanzania's Indigenous Tribes

Nomadic Hadza tribe members in northern Tanzania, above. Opposite, from left: A Barbaig woman; collecting honey from a baobab tree.

ON THE SHORES OF LAKE EYASI, life follows nature's rhythm: the rise and fall of the sun and the periods of dryness and rain. Resting on the edge of the Serengeti Plain, in Tanzania, the area has spectacular, abundant wildlife. But George Mavroudis, proprietor of a namesake safari company, doesn't just bring visitors here for a Land Rover cruise in search of animals. He wants visitors to meet people—specifically, members of the Hadza and Barbaig tribes. Mavroudis aims to give travelers a more personal experience, in part by introducing them to clans who still live intimately with the conditions of the bush, tribes for whom daily sightings of lions or hippopotamuses are matters of significance and concern. (His custom luxury safaris also include game drives.)

The Hadza are hunters and gatherers who have no long-term abodes. When the land begins to get depleted, they move on. Daily life is occupied with meeting survival's basic needs—and it is in these pursuits that visitors accompany

them: foraging for honeycombs high in the branches of a baobab tree or lingering a few paces behind the men as they hunt for dik-diks and impalas using bows and poison-tipped arrows as their weapons.

Unlike the Hadza, whose fly-by-night existence discourages much accumulation of property, the Barbaig keep cattle and live in low, simple houses made of packed-dirt floors and walls of dried mud. At a remote Barbaig village, young men spend the day fetching water for their cows. Bucket after bucket is dragged up into the sun from a well. And when at last their task is finished, the cows make a quiet sound that has echoed down the millennia from biblical days: livestock lapping up water that someone just hoisted out of the ground.

Come the end of the day, there's no TV or radio, no DVD's or computers—just a handful of people sitting around swapping stories as the savannah's night sounds glide in and out of the dark. ✦

For The Guide, see page 277.

MORE CLOSE ENCOUNTERS

In addition to Mavroudis, the following companies also specialize in cultural experiences in Tanzania.
Hoopoe Safaris Runs high-end tours.
IntoAfrica Based in England, offers value-priced excursions.
Cultural Tourism Program Representatives at the tourism office in Arusha can introduce travelers to companies arranging visits with local people.

Cruising Avenida Marginal, Maputo's coastal highway, left. Below: Tongue-searing *piri-piri* prawns at Costa do Sol, a restaurant by the sea. Opposite: Café Camissa.

FLAVORS OF MAPUTO
Eating Out in Mozambique

SUCCULENT MUSSELS, SPICY CURRIES, prawns as big as bananas—Maputo may be known for its pulsing nightlife, but this vibrant multicultural community is also creating some of the most exciting food on the East African coast.

For your first foray into Maputo's culinary world, visit the restaurant Costa do Sol, whose seaside location encourages languid, three-beer lunches. Their tongue-searing *piri-piri* prawns are famous from Cairo to Cape Town. Or, the adventurous can explore the city's cacophonous daily fish market, where fishmongers cajole shoppers into picking from their catch. Walk your selection over to the outdoor cafés lining the market's west end; a vendor will grill it to perfection.

Come evening, stop for a bite at Café Camissa, which functions as a bar–gallery–meeting place. Move on to Clube Naval, a hybrid restaurant, bar, and nautical club that is one of the city's social epicenters. Pair their Zambezi curried chicken with Laurentina, the excellent local lager.

A short ferry ride across the channel from downtown, the Catembe Gallery Hotel is where you'll find Maputo's best alfresco lunch. Try the pizza; the restaurant makes its cheese from the milk of African buffalo. The lobby opens onto a terrace with snapshot-perfect views of the city's skyline. +

For The Guide, see page 277.

Ranger trainees practicing a rescue mission.

WHERE THE CAPE BUFFALO ROAM

Learn to Be a Safari Ranger in South Africa

YOU MAY HAVE WONDERED WHAT TO DO if ever confronted by an angry lion. Do not run for your life. The lion will treat you quite rudely. You can, however, scream at the top of your lungs. "If it's night, though, you're toast," says Mike Karantonis, a veteran CC Africa safari ranger at the Phinda Private Game Reserve, in northeast South Africa. "They rule the night."

Cape buffalo grazing in the Phinda reserve in South Africa, above.

Chobe Chilwero, in Botswana.

RANGER TRAINING 101

Phinda, in the Zulu homeland of Maputaland, is one of the world's most diverse game parks. There are elephants and stink ants, black rhinos and trap-door spiders. It harbors seven types of ecosystem. Few guides can navigate these habitats better than CC Africa safari rangers. The company has the top ranger-training program on the continent, and visitors can sign on for a four-day Bush Skills class to pick up some wilderness know-how, such as weaving a rope strong enough to pull a Land Rover. And it's not all hard work—lodge guests also get wild-mushroom consommés and high-thread-count linens.

A key part of the program is learning to track exotic animals. Ranger trainers lead recruits along trails, teaching them how to differentiate between hippo and rhino prints. (Hippos have four toes, rhinos three.) There are more prints to memorize as well: elephants, Cape buffalo, terrapin, and porcupines.

More exercises follow. One involves practicing a medical evacuation scenario. Another requires rehearsing an encounter with a surly lion (played, nobly, by one of the trainers). The proper reaction is to shout and hold your ground, forcing the animal to retreat. Not everyone succeeds.

Karantonis revels in having the African veld as an office. "One day I saw a lioness sitting on the highest rock in the area, mist around her, a herd of wildebeest below. I thought, *This is it. I'm completely happy.*" In his company, you will be too. ✢

For The Guide, see page 277.

For visitors who think they have what it takes to track a rhino, there are a number of top-of-the-line bush-skills programs in addition to CC Africa's, most of which also put you up in high-end lodges: **Abercrombie & Kent** Private-label guides conduct customized ranger training out of Chobe Chilwero, in Botswana, among other locations. **EcoTraining** The company offers a 28-day course that includes sleep-outs in the bush, habitat management, and tracking the Big Five in South Africa's Kruger Park and Karongwe Camps. **The Bush Camp Company and Mfuwe Lodge** A basic, weeklong course in Zambia covers everything from how to track dangerous prey to finding food and water in the bush.

Helena
Blaunstein,
the owner
of Frau Blau.

Shopping at Delicatessen, a Tel Aviv boutique, left. Below: Jewelry on display at Delicatessen.

ISRAELI INNOVATION

Tel Aviv's Young Designers

THE TEL AVIV NEIGHBORHOOD OF GAN HAHASHMAL takes its name from the city's first "electric park," which opened in the 1920's. Surrounded by manicured greenery and a cluster of late-Ottoman-era houses, the area flourished during Israel's pre-Independence period in the 1940's—before the citywide Bauhaus architectural boom. Now Tel Aviv's indie-fashion crowd has rediscovered the area.

One of the first shops to arrive was Delicatessen. The store's quirky-yet-crafty jewelry, embellished clutches, and high-waisted trousers capture the Gan's unconventional sartorial spirit. Nearby, at Frau Blau (German slang for "drunk woman"), Uzbek-born Helena Blaunstein carries a vintage-inspired women's clothing line with vibrant colors and patchwork patterns. In Shani Bar's tiny namesake boutique, the designer displays her collection, including shoes (from pumps to sandals), roomy purses, and Wrangler-style belts—all created in her second-floor atelier using mostly Italian leathers. And while Nait Rozenfelder's intimate fashion shows have a cultlike following, it's her array of double-collared jackets, kimono-like dresses, and flower-patterned blouses at Nait that steals the scene. +

For The Guide, see page 277.

DUBAI RISING

The Arab World's Postmodern Playground

TOURISM IN DUBAI IS NOT TOURISM AS we know it, but a revved-up, va-va-voom version, and the projects of the developers here would make even Barnum & Bailey blush. In this small city in a tiny emirate on a spit of land that spikes out into the Persian Gulf, there are 10 supersize shopping malls, each larger and more grandiose than the last. One roughly duplicates the Taj Mahal; another houses a black-diamond ski slope. One hotel looks like a boat, another like a sail. Soon to be built: the world's first underwater resort.

Before the discovery of oil, in 1966, Dubai was a sleepy fishing hamlet populated by Bedouin tribesmen, boat makers, and pearl divers. Today it is the playground of kings and sheikhs. Travel to the Nad Al Sheba, Dubai's world-class racetrack, and you'll find horses wearing the royal blue colors of Sheikh Mohammed's renowned Godolphin stables; the nearby stables have a dedicated swimming pool for the horses. Head along the highway and you'll see—off in the distance, down a security-monitored boulevard—a palace that belongs to one of the many sheikhs. Drive to the desert and you'll end up at Bab Al Shams, a sandy resort.

Shopping, not sightseeing, is the real passion of visitors. At the Mall of the Emirates, with boutiques from Marc Jacobs and Burberry, as well

The city of Dubai, an emerging international destination rising from the desert, left.

Shopping at the Mall of the Emirates, above. Opposite: A customized car in Dubai.

as a branch of Harvey Nichols, women in long black *abbayahs* clutch designer purses. Some of their robes are studded with rhinestones at the hem—subtle fashion statements.

The hotel resorts—Al Qasr, the Park Hyatt, the One & Only Royal Mirage—are all magnificent. At around $2,000 per night, a standard double at the self-proclaimed "seven-star" Burj Al Arab costs about what the workers who built the resort make in a year. You can have a personal butler arrange aromatherapy for you in the comfort of your own whirlpool. (Your butler will also do your unpacking.) The rooms are decorated with huge amounts of gilt; deep reds, royal blues, and bright yellows; velvets, satins, tassels, and buttons. The furniture is idiosyncratic, oversize, curved, and elongated, as if designed by the love child of Salvador Dalí and Antoni Gaudí.

Beyond the manufactured luxury, Dubai is a refuge from the strictures of the rest of the Islamic world; people come here not just for the business but for the freedom. At Sho Cho, a restaurant and nightclub, the women

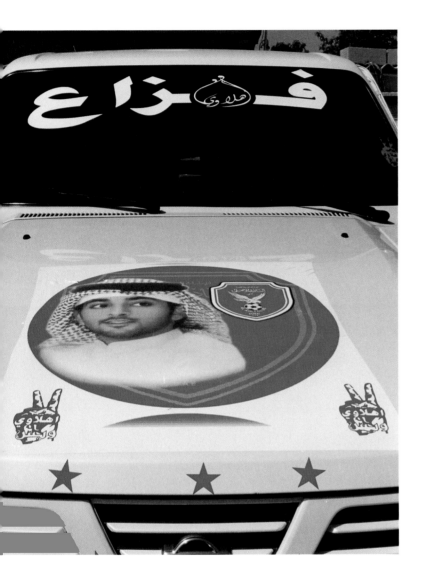

wear anything but traditional dress. People converse in English. Most of them are from Lebanon, but some are Egyptian or Saudi; others are from Bahrain, Oman, or Europe.

Reminders of what is to come are everywhere. Soon, the tallest building in the world, a slender needle of daunting grace called Burj Dubai, will dominate a skyline that is already famously postmodern. As you drive down Sheikh Zayed Road, flanked by skyscrapers in unimaginable proportions, banners for the future tower flap from the streetlights. One after another, they proclaim: BURJ DUBAI—HISTORY RISING. +

For The Guide, see page 277.

DON'T MISS STOPS IN DUBAI

There's no shortage of high-gloss shopping in Dubai. Head to these standout boutiques and galleries:

Five Green This concept store/gallery holds art shows and performances, and sells casual clothes from young designers.

Harvey Nichols Opened in 2006, this marble-bedecked complex houses a good selection of designer labels—and the Almaz restaurant, from Mourad "Momo" Mazouz.

S*uce A fashion boutique that's unique for Dubai (you can enter directly from the street), with clothes by international and Middle Eastern designers.

Third Line This gallery exhibits everything from photography to video art and organizes film screenings.

Villa Moda A luxury shopping destination in the Jumeirah Emirates Towers from Kuwait's "sheikh of chic," Majed al-Sabah.

XVA Contemporary art by home-grown talent, plus a vegetarian café.

ON SAND AND SEA

Exploring the Wilds of Oman

ITS VERY NAME EVOKES THE EXOTICISM of the unexplored. Within the small sultanate of Oman, which is roughly the size of Kansas, endless sands and pristine seas lie in close proximity. The many varied expanses contain countless adventures: trips to *wadis* where one can swim through semi-subterranean pools to find immense cave systems; visits to remote turtle hatcheries in a protected and little-visited region in the north; camel-trekking expeditions through the desert.

Adjectives such as *splendid* and *stupendous* hardly exaggerate the beauty of the coastline, particularly one stretch south of the

Setting out on the bay from the Barr Al Jissah resort in Oman, left. Below: Taking in the view of the Gulf of Oman. Opposite: A dune in the Wahiba Sands, south of Barr Al Jissah.

capital. There, Shangri-La's Barr Al Jissah resort complex is set on talcum-white sand between two rocky points. Swimmers find turquoise waters teeming with schools of clown-colored fish. The marine life is exceptional: on boat rides in the Gulf of Oman, you are almost guaranteed to see dolphins romping in cavorting posses. Colors here stand in contrast: the flat yolk of the sun, the biscuit-colored cliffs, the glistening blue-gray of whales as they crest to drink the air.

In the desert interior, a starker beauty is on display. Oman is, and remains in many ways, an antique land, and maps are startlingly blank. A few principal highways are intersected by dotted lines that, in some cases, indicate camel trails. The Wahiba Sands extend for thousands of square miles; there, you'll find a David Lean landscape of fantastic mountains, chiefly pink-orange in color but also, in places, a mottled fawn and rose-red and, where shadows blanket the dunes, an enveloping deep brown. The barrenness is deceptive. Things live in the sand, creatures that camouflage themselves against desert colors, avoiding the brutal light of daytime and appearing in their multitudes only by night. Bedouin nomads are said to still inhabit the dunes.

Some entrepreneurs, among them descendants of the Bedouin, run jeep tours of the dunes, and most major hotels can arrange trips. Indeed, it would be unwise to venture out without an experienced guide well-supplied with water and food. Added to the risks are the desert drivers, who see flying off dunes as sport, gunning the engine for the edge, driving into what appears to be sheer space. ✛

For The Guide, see page 277.

ASIA

The neighborhood Bukit Bintang, Kuala Lumpur's shopping hub.

MONGOLIAN HEIGHTS

Tour Temples in a Far-Flung Land

ALTHOUGH SURROUNDED BY GIANTS, Mongolia itself is no slouch. With its stark, ravishing landscapes and resurgent Buddhist traditions, the country is at last emerging from the long shadow of Soviet Communism. Residents are once again celebrating a unique culture, with traces of Chinese and Russian influence, as well as the glorious history of the Mongols, who established one of the world's great empires.

Change is most evident in the country's monasteries. Much like Tibet, Mongolia was an ecclesiastical state in the pre-Communist era. (The Dalai Lama's ancestry can be traced back to a 16th-century Mongolian ruler.) Until the 20th century, Buddhism was woven into the fabric of everyday life, its rituals and mantras ever present during marriages and funerals. When the Communists took over, countless monasteries were destroyed, but more than 100 have reopened since 1990, and the number of monks is increasing.

A tented *ger* camp outside Kharkorin.

A herder on horseback in the Mongolian countryside, above left. Above right: The Choijin Lama Monastery, in Ulaanbaatar.

The true face of contemporary Mongolian Buddhism can be seen at Gandan monastery, which is now home to more than 500 monks, in the capital of Ulaanbaatar. Monks who fled to India, Europe, and America have returned; they are training others and practicing the traditional Buddhist art of *thangka* painting. Inside Migjid Janraisig Sum, the main temple in the monastery complex, pilgrims bow before the 85-foot-high gilded statue of Avalokiteshwara. Also in Ulaanbaatar, the Choijin Lama Monastery—a classic example of traditional Buddhist architecture—has upturned tile roofs that shelter a collection of *tsam* dancing masks.

Reaching the 16th-century Erdene Zuu Khiid, Mongolia's oldest monastery, requires traveling deep into the remote countryside to the ancient capital of Karakorum. For many miles on the long straight road, there are no other vehicles or human beings in sight, just sky and undulating grassland. Occasionally, white spots appear on the hills, which reveal themselves as *gers*—the white circular tents that are the Mongolian version of the Central Asian yurt.

Originally built from the ruins of the capital, Erdene Zuu Khiid has been razed and rebuilt many times. Its vast walled compound, which feels deserted, is entered through gates with floating

A monk in a *ger* temple in Ulaanbaatar, above left. Above right: The central Mongolian landscape. Opposite: Worshippers gather before a statue of Buddha at the Gandan monastery, in Ulaanbaatar.

T+L Tip

Mongolia's rapid development means rapid change: work has begun on a 1,650-mile highway that will bring industry to the Gobi Desert. It will be finished in 2010— so visit the country now, before the road is completed.

Chinese eaves. Chapels housing the Buddha statues are under lock and key, and the temple shadows lie sharp on the ground.

Karakorum itself was built by Genghis Khan's son and successor, Ögödei. The city (now called Kharkorin) was once the seat of extraordinary power and known in places as far away as India and Iran. Marco Polo mentions it in an account of his travels. Abandoned in the 13th century, when the capital was moved to what is now Beijing, all that's left of Karakorum today are four turtle-shaped rocks. Encircled and diminished by Russian and Chinese powers, and waiting for Western tourists and investors, modern Mongolia seems very far from its adventurous past. And the ruins of Karakorum make the transience and impermanence of human glory all the easier to grasp. ✛

For The Guide, see page 278.

大连市商业银行

MODERN MANCHURIA

Cityscapes of Northeast China

ONCE A WILD AND UNTAMED TERRITORY, inhabited by nomads and ruled by warlords, Manchuria—now known simply as Northeast China—is a cosmopolitan blend of Russian, Chinese, Manchu, Korean, and Japanese influences.

The modern history of Manchuria is mostly a story about railways. Even today, the best way to get a feel for the region's cities is to take the train from Dalian in the south to Harbin, along the Harbin-Dalian Railway line.

Dalian is often described as the

A public square in Dalian, in northeast China. Opposite: Bicycling through Shenyang, the largest city in Manchuria.

Hong Kong of the North. Originally a Chinese fishing village, it was turned into a graceful city, modeled after Paris, by the Russians. Later, the Japanese left their mark and took cues from the Westernized Tokyo of the 1920's and 30's. The shopping malls (with names like Victory Plaza), high-rise hotels, and brand-new office buildings are mostly copies of structures in Hong Kong and Singapore, icons of modernity. That is what gives Dalian and other Manchurian cities their peculiar flavor: the dreams of someplace else, someplace grander.

The largest city in the northeast is Shenyang (formerly Mukden). Traveling there by train, you'll probably go over the same bit of track destroyed by Japanese soldiers on September 18, 1931, in the so-called Mukden Incident, which led to the Japanese military occupation of the whole of Manchuria. The 9.18 Museum in Shenyang, with the legend "9.18" on its façade, commemorates the event with photographs, sound effects, and wax tableaux. The historically minded can also visit the Ch'ing dynasty palace and the mansion of the warlord Zhang Zuolin and his son, Zhang Xueliang, who was known as much for his ballroom-dancing skills as for his violent acts.

Changchun is perhaps the least glamorous but most fascinating of Manchuria's major cities. The Japanese transformed it into Shinkyo, the

A couple strolls through the Victory Plaza Mall, in Dalian, above.
Left: The 9:18 Museum in Shenyang.

capital of their puppet state, with straight, wide avenues and huge official buildings in the "New Asian" style. The display of architectural bombast was also congenial to the Chinese Communist Party, which established its headquarters there after the revolution in 1949.

Traveling on from Changchun to Harbin, you already feel the vastness of Siberia, a few hundred miles away. This area used to be so populated with bandits that Japanese trains stopped running at nightfall. After the Russian Revolution, Harbin, a refuge for more than 400,000 White Russians, was known for its churches. The most beautiful, wooden St. Nicholas, was destroyed during the Cultural Revolution, but red-brick St. Sophia, in the center of town, remains. On the shopping street Zhongyang Avenue (formerly Kitaiskaya), old restaurants still display some of the ornate elegance of the 1920's. One of the street's landmarks, the Hotel Moderne, is worth a look. Another reason to come to Zhongyang Avenue is to eat steamed or fried dumplings, a northern Chinese delicacy.

Time has made these places more attractive, and lent them a certain stylishness. In a sense, the modern Chinese are continuing the dream started by their former occupiers: to transform the region into a series of glitzy cities. ✤

For The Guide, see page 278.

DIM SUM DELIGHT

The Food of Guangzhou

GUANGZHOU, IN SOUTHEASTERN CHINA, is the center of Cantonese cooking, and it's easy to see why locals are so fiercely loyal to it. Forget what you've heard about Hong Kong's food being the best; when it comes to dim sum, Guangzhou is unrivaled. Rise early for the best selections at the Garden Hotel's Peach Blossom restaurant: sesame balls, fried taro puffs with crab, and rice noodles with pork. Waitresses in gold-and-white uniforms pour fragrant chrysanthemum tea.

At Yumin, the largest and most famous of the city's pick-what-you-eat, live-seafood restaurants, dozens of tanks filled with giant lobsters and Mandarin fish line the walls. Four-foot-long alligators roam the front dining room, their mouths tied shut with twine. (You can order one for dinner.) The restaurant's array of sweets—fried peanut crêpes; buttercream pastries; *dofu fa*, a sweet silky-tofu dessert—is almost as spectacular.

Guangzhou is, most of all, a market town. At Qingping Market, the alleys are ripe for foraging. There's dried everything, along with loose teas, lotus root, and live eels. It's the place to feel the city's rhythm, where bargaining is a staccato dance of words. +

For The Guide, see page 278.

Yumin restaurant, on the outskirts of Guangzhou. Above: Dumplings at Peach Blossom restaurant.

BUILDING BOOM

The Casino Culture in Macau

FAST ON ITS WAY TO BECOMING THE LAS VEGAS of the Far East, Macau is filling up with spectacular, over-the-top casinos. Although the flood of international gaming money is a recent phenomenon, gambling has been one of its attractions since the mid 19th century. As Hong Kong became a booming global trading post, Macau, a backwater run by a lesser colonial power—Portugal—faded. But after World War II, its reputation for casinos and related activities grew.

One of the most significant entries is Wynn Resorts, which opened its casino and 600-room hotel on the Avenida da Amizade in 2006. Its Macau casino is a bronzed-glass wedge much like the Wynn Las Vegas, but it is surrounded by two stories of faux Portuguese-colonial architecture. "We are not creating a new Las Vegas in Macau," insists Grant Bowie, president and general manager of Wynn Resorts Macau. "What we're creating is a new Macau."

The Macau skyline. Opposite, clockwise from top left: Construction on the Cotai Strip; at Fisherman's Wharf, a waterfront shopping mall; Macau's central square.

But, like Vegas, Macau now offers plenty of excess—much of it copied from elsewhere. On Avenida da Amizade, a boulevard lined with vintage gambling palaces, there is the 165,000-square-foot gold glass–clad Sands. The Hotel Lisboa, nearby, is topped with what appears to be a giant roulette wheel; its interior is Morris Lapidus meets Louis XIV. At Fisherman's Wharf, a waterfront shopping mall, stores and restaurants are set in replicas of ancient Rome, Miami, New Orleans, and Lisbon; a fake volcano houses a roller coaster and a Victorian-style hotel.

The building boom is hardly over. Eight huge developments are taking shape on the Cotai Strip, a three-quarter-mile sliver of reclaimed land. A version of the Las Vegas Venetian Casino Resort—which will include a wave pool and a rooftop putting course—is set to open this year and to look somewhat like Venice by way of Nevada. Other casinos, many built by the Sands, as well as hotels managed by the Four Seasons and Shangri-la, will be "Portuguese-contemporary-colonial" or "Tibetan-feel" or "Tuscany-maybe." Perhaps Macau's most avant-garde complex is in the works: the City of Dreams, which will include a "tropical underwater casino hall."

Much of the development in Macau is elaborate stagecraft, intended to lure the masses. After all, there are 1.3 billion potential tourists and gamblers just across Macau's inner harbor. ✚

For The Guide, see page 278.

The terrace at the Utoco Deep
Sea Therapy Center & Hotel,
on the Japanese island of
Shikoku, left. The resort's
reading room, above. Opposite,
from left: A bowl of rice
porridge; the hotel's walkway.

TAKE THE WATERS

A Healing Spa on Japan's Shikoku Island

AT THE 17-ROOM Utoco Deep Sea Therapy Center & Hotel,
on the easternmost tip of Japan's subtropical Shikoku island,
beauty maestro Shu Uemura is harnessing uncontaminated
deep-sea water for its therapeutic value. Rich in potassium,
calcium, and magnesium, this special water has other trace ele-
ments missing from surface water. And according to Uemura,
it can have positive effects on digestion and skin tone.

At Utoco, pools are filled with water pumped up from the
ocean depths; many of the beauty products, treatments, and
even meals are infused with it. If all this sounds a bit far-out,
that's because this is the first spa of its kind, although similar

experiments are taking place on coastlines from Norway to Tahiti.

Built on pylons behind a breakwater, the Modernist concrete-and-steel resort sits between the surf and a steep hillside. The Tokyo- and Paris-based design firm Ciel Rouge devised the single-level structure so that it arcs horizontally along the shore, ensuring that wherever you sit (on deck chaises, at dining tables, in bed), your view of the Pacific is unobstructed. Upon arrival, relax on a low couch and watch fishing boats navigate the bubbling brine, then wander along Utoco's sheltered deck, where every curve reveals another intentionally framed scene.

Venture into the ovoid spa or dip into the indoor pool, where the deep-sea water, heated to body temperature, has an effervescent quality that can't be credited solely to the underwater jets. Wind up in the outdoor whirlpool and watch the Pacific slosh upward against brown volcanic rocks while you contemplate its bottom 11,480 feet below. After long soaks in Utoco's fizzy pools, you may notice a sea change of your own. ✚

For The Guide, see page 278.

JAPAN'S LAST FRONTIER

The Natural Wonders of Hokkaido

A LAND OF WIDE-OPEN SPACES, sprawling cattle ranches, and pioneer spirit, Hokkaido is the Japanese version of the Wild West. For Americans, the country's northernmost island poses a dramatic contrast with what is often imagined to be the "real Japan"—the decorous temples of Nara and Kyoto, for example, or the historic cities of Kyushu.

Hokkaido also happens to be the country's least densely populated island. Large swaths of it are wild, bleak, and windy; brown bears roam freely and sea eagles glide over the water in search of prey. The people who live here today are descendants of the first settlers from Japan, who came in the 19th century to provide a buffer against Russia. Some of them were hardy idealists, others were desperadoes looking for a fresh start.

Winter, when temperatures rarely rise above 30 degrees and snow and freezing conditions prevail, is perhaps the most spectacular, if unlikely, time to travel here. Since major highways are kept passable, driving isn't as risky as it sounds, and most rental cars have snow tires and chains. On the road inland from the small town of Abashiri to Lake Akan, you'll pass

The Windsor Hotel in Hokkaido, Japan's northernmost island, above.
Right, from top: Birch trees in the snow; a road sign near the
northern coast. Opposite: A view of Lake Toya, on the southwestern part
of the island, from inside the Windsor Hotel.

through unforgettable scenery: frozen lakes and geysers spouting jets of scalding water over the snow; whooper swans landing like miniature Concordes; red-crowned cranes (once a delicacy served to the Emperor, as his royal prerogative) dancing for prospective mates in the wetlands. In midwinter the bears are all asleep, but in the warmer seasons, hikers are advised to wear bells around their necks; startled bears can be especially dangerous.

After making your way through this harsh landscape, the Windsor Hotel Toya Resort & Spa, overlooking Lake Toya, comes as a welcome respite from the cold. The isolated hotel sits like a gleaming cruise ship above Toya's shore, all soaring glass lobbies and airy rooms with downy beds dressed in crisp white. The surrounding Shikotsu-Toya National Park can be explored on horseback, and there's skiing nearby. But the hotel is most famous as an *onsen* (Japanese hot spring) resort. There's nothing quite like slipping into hot spring water in the open air at night, after an afternoon of skiing, a good meal, and a warm sake. ✢

For The Guide, see page 279.

A PALACE AFFAIR

Central India's Royal Past

Sculptured stonework of the Lakshmana Temple in Khajuraho, India, left. Below: The Jai Vilas Palace Museum in Gwalior. Opposite: A monument on the bank of the Betwa River, in Orchha.

AFTER STOPPING IN AGRA for a look at the World's Greatest Monument to Love (a.k.a. the Taj Mahal), most visitors proceed apace to India's other big-name destinations: the sacred city of Varanasi or the breathtaking scenery in the region of Kerala. If you want to lose the crowds, it's worth taking a detour along the dusty back roads of the neighboring states to explore off-the-radar temples and palaces, some of which have been converted into hotels.

Just 90 minutes from Agra is the city of Dholpur, home to the Raj Niwas Palace. Built in 1876, under the patronage of the great-grandfather of the current owner, the palace today is a hotel filled with animal trophies; its towering interiors are lavished to the ceiling with custom-made majolica tiles from Europe. The owner's mother, Vasundhara Raje,

happens to be chief minister of Rajasthan and a part-time resident at the hotel, so you may pass her in the hall on the way to breakfast.

Raje's father is the Maharajah Jivaji Rao Scindia, and their ancestors once ruled the nearby city of Gwalior, located an hour and a half south of Dholpur. In 1875, the Scindias built the Usha Kiran Palace, now a hotel, to receive the overflow (including the retinue of Britain's Queen Mary) from their adjoining Jai Vilas Palace. One part of the Jai Vilas palace, where the

Colored powders for devotional ceremonies, in the town of Orchha, left. Above: One of the many monuments built for former rulers in Orchha.

prince still lives, has been turned into a museum, in which visitors are invited to ponder the meaning of a crystal staircase. The maharajah's palace is a trifle compared with Gwalior's 15th-century fortress, planted on a ridge 300 feet above the city and the real reason for stopping over. The Man Mandir, within this citadel, is the finest, best-preserved example of an early Hindu palace in all of India.

Three hours from Gwalior, the Betwa River slips like a noose around the medieval island palaces of Orchha.

Amazingly, one of them—the Jehangir Mahal, a monument to Indo-Islamic architecture—has a hotel, the Sheesh Mahal, within its walls. In the hotel, the Maharaja and Maharani suites are vaults of comfort, without being self-consciously fancy. When the few visiting tourists go home at the end of the day, overnight guests have the Jehangir to themselves, and can wander around at will in the moonlight.

Four hours stand between Orchha and the famously erotic carvings of Khajuraho's Hindu temples, constructed in the 10th and 11th centuries. The best place to stay in the village is the Chandela, a Taj Hotel that unintentionally recalls the glamour of Miami's first Golden Period. It's the splendor of two different places effortlessly commingling. ✛

For The Guide, see page 279.

LONG LEGACY

The Rich History of Sri Lanka's Golden Triangle

THE SMALL ISLAND OF SRI LANKA— which, to borrow the words of Sri Lankan–born novelist Michael Ondaatje, falls on a map below India in the shape of a tear—was the location of some of the world's earliest Buddhist kingdoms, and its shrines are correspondingly important. Many of them are clustered in the Golden Triangle, an area whose perimeter connects

The ruins of Sigiriya, a fortress built in the fourth century, in Sri Lanka's Golden Triangle.

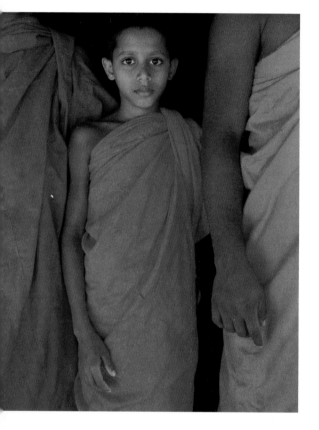

An 11-year-old monk at Sigiriya, left. Above: The 18th-century Temple of the Tooth, in Kandy. Opposite, clockwise from top left: Students on recess in Dambulla; a view of the hills in Kandy; an elephant on the grounds of the Kandalama Hotel.

Kandy to Anuradhapura and Polonnaruwa, in the center of the island.

Driving from the capital city of Colombo north to Kandy, you'll pass through the island's storied plantations, each seemingly given over to a specific spice: peppers, cinnamon, cloves, and other culinary aromatics that for centuries lured the world to this small, rich spot in the faraway Indian Ocean. Kandy itself was the last pre-Colonial capital of the former Sinhalese kingdom, and its most famous attraction is the Temple of

the Tooth. Erected in the 18th century to guard the Buddha's sacred molar, the pink temple is open 24 hours a day. Pad barefoot around gilded antechambers to the sanctum sanctorum, where, according to myth, the Buddha's tooth is enshrined. A more worldly paradise is found at the nearby Peradeniya Botanic Gardens, with its improbable Hollywood avenues of Royal Palms—specimen trees planted by 19th-century European nobility touring the colonies—and immense mangroves filled with clamoring fruit bats.

At Dambulla, stone steps rise 500 feet through rock face to five great cave temples dating back to the first century B.C., each ornamented with fresco cycles and statuary that depict episodes in the Buddha's life in serial sitcom form. With more than 2,100 square feet of mural paintings, it's the

largest cave-temple compound in the country.

Kandalama, a great hotel designed in the 1990's by famed Sri Lankan architect Geoffrey Bawa, is nearby. Few structures are more sensitively fitted to their setting than this one, a building nestled like a multistory honeycomb against a cliff and roofed with sod. Its hundreds of windowed chambers are oriented to views across a vast lake dug manually 800 years ago. Vines cloak the façade of the building. Troupes of gray langur monkeys swing from the struts. Come nightfall, small bats carom along the ceilings of stucco corridors cut from the stone of the cliff.

In the medieval town of Polonnaruwa, the ruins of Sri Lanka's 13th-century capital can be toured on foot or by bicycle. The complex of crumbling buildings spreads over several

T+L Tip

A long-running civil war is still being fought in Sri Lanka. Though the violence level fluctuates, it is largely contained to the country's north. At press time, there was no official travel advisory for Sri Lanka, but to stay updated on current events, log on to the U.S. State Department Web site, travel.state.gov.

The view of the pool and the reservoir from the Kandalama Hotel, left. Below: Flower delivery. Opposite: Dambulla's Golden Buddha Temple.

acres of grass and gravel; the Royal Palace is roofless, but the 12-foot-thick walls still rise impressively. All that's left of the Atadage—the original Temple of the Tooth—are stairs leading to rows of imposing stone pillars.

Another great day trip from the Kandalama is Sigiriya, a vertiginous rock outcrop 560 feet above swaths of manicured fields and groves, topped by a fifth-century palace of the same name. At the lowest level sits a series of cool, shaded gardens surrounding symmetrical water channels designed according to a complex system of hydraulics. Visitors climb by stages along zigzagging stairs that lie between the colossal sculpted paws of a lion (the name *Sigiriya* is thought to be a corruption of *Simha-giri,* or "lion mountain"). Midway up, rock walls, accessed by a rickety catwalk, are painted with ancient, sensual frescoes.

No one knows the meaning of this small grouping of elegant creatures, sometimes deemed *Apsaras*, or celestial beings. Who were these topless lovelies toting trays of fruit? Prostitutes, or temple maidens captured as they processed to a shrine nearby? Up on top of Sigiriya rock are the ruins of the palace, less compelling somehow than the views of the horizon across a viridescent jungle composed of a thousand greens— a vision that makes the world appear miraculous, if precious and fleeting. +

For The Guide, see page 279.

A local child in front of St. Joseph's Cathedral, in Hanoi, above. Opposite, from top: Lamps for sale along a Hanoi street; touring a temple in Hanoi.

ASIA FOR ALL AGES

A Family Trip to Vietnam

WITH ITS ENDLESS SIGHTS—pagodas, water-puppet shows, exotic candy shops—kids will never complain of being bored in Vietnam. In the cities, fruit sellers carry baskets of mandarin oranges on poles balanced across their shoulders, old ladies dish up noodles from sidewalk stands, and motorbikes roar by. And the countryside is perfect for bicycling and boating excursions.

Hanoi, the 1,000-year-old capital, is a good place to start, and a handy base for side trips. For a thrilling street-level tour, pack the family into a cyclo, the Vietnamese pedicab. The Hai Ba Trung area has century-old European-style villas, and Hoan Kiem is given over to crowded markets (fresh tofu! live snakes!). The mazelike streets of the Old Quarter are full

of tinsel streamers, and the shops on Hang Thang (Charcoal-Sellers' Street) are famous for the local candy called *banh com*, a type of sweet cake.

If Hanoi is Vietnam's Washington, D.C., then brash Ho Chi Minh City (formerly Saigon) is the nation's Los Angeles. Pick a central base, such as the Caravelle Hotel, and duck back in for breaks from the midday heat. Pay a visit to Cho Lon and light incense at the elaborate Quan Am Pagoda. At

The Cai Rang floating market along Vietnam's Mekong Delta. Left: Candied fruits in Hanoi.

4 REASONS KIDS LOVE VIETNAM

1. Cyclos Take a spin in a pedicab. Set the rate before riding—$2 is typical for an hour—and remember to tip.

2. Pagodas and Temples Visit on full- or new-moon days, when Buddhists come to light incense and pray.

3. Pickup Soccer Local children spend their park time caught up in *bong da* (soccer); they'll be thrilled if your kids join in.

4. Custom Tailors Let your junior fashionistas design outfits at one of Vietnam's affordable tailors. In Hanoi, shops on Hang Gai Street specialize in silk: Le Minh Silk is a good bet. For other fabrics, try VIS Fashion.

night, take a dinner cruise along the Saigon River, looking out at the tall buildings and flashing neon.

Outside the major cities, head to the Mekong Delta for a motorboat tour of the river, where waterways are crowded with narrow sampans weighted with coconuts and grape-sized longan fruit, a delicacy known as "dragon's eyes." Explore the roads on mountain bikes, gliding past rice fields and prim, colorful houses. You're likely to attract a greeting committee of friendly village kids, dashing to the road to call out "Hello!"

The best way to experience Ha Long Bay, a series of 1,600 limestone islands spread across nearly 600 miles of the Gulf of Tonkin, is aboard a wooden junk, a traditional Chinese boat with graceful sails. The islands jut out dramatically from the turquoise water. Stop for the night at Cat Ba Island, and climb one of the vertiginous peaks in Cat Ba National Park. At the end of your stay in Vietnam, the kids will swagger like adventurers who've explored some magical, far-off land. +

For The Guide, see page 279.

FACING THE FUTURE

The New Energy of Kuala Lumpur

BENEATH ITS *BLADE RUNNER* SURFACE, Kuala Lumpur is a place where dizzying development and multiculturalism collide. With its warp-speed economic progress and its unusual mix of Malays, Chinese, and Indians, Malaysia's capital is experiencing rapid change. Stroll down the main shopping drag, Bukit Bintang (Star Hill), and you'll see the transformation firsthand.

All of the planet's best-known hotel chains are represented, complete with glittering marble lobbies. The restaurants—Senses in the Hilton, Third Floor in the JW Marriott Hotel—are turning out cuisine to rival New York's. And in the luxury shopping centers, silk-gowned Chinese matrons, turbaned Sikhs, and burka-draped

One of the Petronas Twin Towers, in Kuala Lumpur.

Kuala Lumpur's National Mosque, above. Opposite, from top: Inside Senses restaurant in the Hilton; Sri Kandaswamy Kovil, a Hindu temple.

Muslims elbow one another for Prada and Gucci.

Along the Beach Club strip, velvet-rope nightclubs like Bar Ibiza and Zouk blast hip-hop until the early-morning hours as young girls in tight jeans and bare midriffs gyrate through the cigarette smoke. Occasional raids are carried out by the Religious Department (the sharia courts that deal with noncriminal matters for Muslims), but the crowds don't seem to care. Their flaunting of the rules typifies the electrified atmosphere.

The 21st century hits you at the Kuala Lumpur City Center, in the form of the Petronas Twin Towers. Created by Cesar Pelli, this pair of 88-story skyscrapers looks like rockets on a launchpad. Inside is one of Asia's biggest shopping malls.

Every building within miles seems to have sprung up in the last 20 years, or is currently being erected. Even religious sites, like the National Mosque, with its all-white geometry, feel updated. But there are a few reminders of Malaysia's not-so-distant past: in the architecture of the Hindu temple Sri Kandaswamy Kovil, or on the wide verandas of the British governor's former residence, a rambling two-story mansion that has been turned into the Carcosa Seri Negara hotel. At the Long Bar of the faux-Tudor Selangor Club, a Kuala Lumpur institution more than 120 years old, Somerset Maugham overheard gossip he later used as material for his stories. Visitors come to catch a whiff of the clubhouse's history, but most don't stay long, preferring to flock back to the shops, clubs, and restaurants downtown. ✛

For The Guide, see page 279.

The Esplanade Theatres on the Bay in Singapore, above. Below: The rooftop bar Loof. Opposite: Revitalized Clarke Quay, which teems with nightspots.

ASIA'S NEW DESIGN HUB Stylish Singapore

SINGAPORE, IT SEEMS, IS FINALLY LETTING its hair down. Long considered an island of conformity, the city has planted itself firmly on the global style map. Since the new century began, the city's once-clinical façade has been exhibiting signs of distinctive character. There's a fresh crop of radical buildings, including the Esplanade Theatres on the Bay complex, with its controversial, spiked, durian-like exterior, and Sir Norman Foster's titanium-clad Supreme Court, which hovers like a flying saucer over the skyline.

The formerly neglected area of Club Street and Ann Siang Hill, in Chinatown, has been colonized by energetic young entrepreneurs. At Front Row, the ground-floor tea salon is stocked with Dean & Deluca products; one flight up are handpicked fashions from Kim Jones, A.P.C., and Fab & Jo; and above that is an art gallery. Around the corner, Vanilla Home caters to well-heeled homemakers, with designs by William Yeoward and London society stalwart Nicholas Haslam. Nearby is Asylum Studio, an eclectic concept store where you can buy anything from Holga "Cat Face" cameras to Hussein Chalayan perfume. And Style Nordic carries only Scandinavian wares, from Finnish

Iittala ceramics to Nudie jeans.

At the rooftop bar Loof, the elevator doors part to reveal a vast deck that's open to the sky and surrounded on all sides by the neon-lit cityscape. One wing is encased in glass and padded with private daybeds and ottomans where fashionable young things lounge under the stars. Resin walls are decorated with whimsical silhouettes—a flying baby, a *Psycho*-esque shower scene, and a Clark Kent–Superman figure.

In Rochester Park, the former houses of the colony's civil servants have been reborn as restaurants and bars. The standout is Graze, which serves upmarket brasserie food courtesy of chef Matthew Lawdorn, from Melbourne. You can eat either in the concrete-and-pale-wood environs of the downstairs restaurant or under the outdoor pavilion flanked by tropical gardens. On weekend nights the grounds double as an intimate outdoor cinema with black-and-white films projected onto a freestanding wall in the garden. Likewise, Clarke Quay is a revitalized riverside strip of late-night spots. The rows of former shop houses have been updated with futuristic sunshades courtesy of design firm Arup, and there's a vibrant nightlife scene at clubs like Ministry of Sound.

Nothing embodies the modern-day Singapore aesthetic better than its boutique hotels. Case in point: the New Majestic, with its array of 30 guest rooms—no two the same—done up like a bordello, or a Manhattan studio, or a shagadelic bachelor pad. +

For The Guide, see page 279.

Dining at Graze, in Singapore's Rochester Park, above. Below: T-shirts for sale at Front Row. Opposite: The New Majestic Hotel, Singapore's latest boutique property.

PARADISE FOUND

Travelers Come Back to Bali

The Ku De Ta Restaurant Bar, in the town of Seminyak, above left. Above right: Inside a villa at the Bulgari Resort, outside Ulu Watu. Opposite: A woman walks by a water temple in the northwest part of the island.

DESPITE A FAIR AMOUNT OF RECENT TURBULENCE, hoteliers are still betting on Bali, long one of the world's iconic vacation destinations, by opening a host of luxury properties. Pansea unveiled Ubud Hanging Gardens, set in a dramatic Ayung River gorge. Bulgari Hotels' cliff-top, all-villa resort debuted near Ulu Watu; the Como Shambhala Estate, in Begawan, was redeveloped as a stunning holistic spa; and a St. Regis is on the horizon. Restaurateurs, too, are bringing new energy to the serene island ringed with beaches. In the upscale town of Seminyak, lovely seaside tables are set up nightly at La Lucciola and Ku De Ta Restaurant Bar. And R. Aja's (which was targeted in the 2005 attacks) has reopened in an airy second-floor space. Bali, it seems, has rebounded. +

For The Guide, see page 280.

T+L Tip

For current security information, check the U.S. State Department's Web site at travel.state. gov. The United Kingdom's Foreign & Commonwealth Office is also an excellent resource for travel advice (fco.gov.uk), and Bali Discovery Tours (balidiscovery.com) produces an objective and useful roundup of island news every week.

Te Whau Vineyard, on New Zealand's Waiheke Island.

AUSTRALIA + NEW ZEALAND + THE SOUTH PACIFIC

BOHO CHIC

The Aussie Hideaway
of Byron Bay

FOR DECADES, BYRON BAY WAS KNOWN IN AUSTRALIA as an outpost for the cosmic crowd, brimming with trinket shops that sold tie-dyed shirts and crystals. But now the town—a 90-minute flight from Sydney—is trading hippie for hip with a clutch of stylish hotels, restaurants, and shops.

The poshest addition is the Byron at Byron Resort & Spa, a Balinese-style property in a rain forest. Guests can bike to their suites along raised walkways, practice yoga by the infinity pool, or dine in the alfresco restaurant. Those who value privacy as much as 800-thread-count sheets should look to the four-bedroom Byron Bay Villa, an oceanfront rental on Watego's Beach. The town's original glam hotel, Rae's on Watego's, recently

Tallow Beach, on the south end of Byron Bay. Opposite: Relaxing downtown.

The living room of Byron Bay Villa, a 20-minute walk from the center of town.

T+L Tip

Surfers brave Byron Bay's waves year-round, but the best weather is from December through March. In June and July, and again in September and November, the headlands are ideal for whale-watching, as breaching humpbacks fill the surrounding waters.

reopened after a luxe makeover. The Mediterranean-meets-Moroccan space has just six rooms and a poolside villa.

Jonson Street, Byron Bay's main thoroughfare, is dotted with surf shops and sleek restaurants. With its all-white décor and sexy, often shoeless patrons, Dish evokes South Beach style—but not the diet. The menu includes smoked salmon–stuffed peppers in a creamy romesco sauce.

For smooth seas, head to the tranquil Belongil Bay, just west of town. The dramatic coastline views along the winding path to the century-old Cape Byron Lighthouse are worth the hike—especially early in the morning, when you can catch the sunrise. ✦

For The Guide, see page 280.

Goat cheese pizza at Apple Bar, in the town of Bilpin, left. Below: Apple Bar chef Michael Jaggard.

GASTRONOMIC HEIGHTS

The Cuisine of Australia's Blue Mountains

OF THE HUNDREDS OF THOUSANDS OF TRAVELERS who visit the Blue Mountains in New South Wales each year, most come for bushwalking, garden tours, ethereal views, and to visit the Three Sisters rock formation near the busy Art Deco town of Katoomba. Still, many manage to miss one of the area's best attractions: an innovative food scene.

Tourism has been big business in these mountains 60 miles northwest of Sydney ever since the first rail line between Penrith and Wentworth Falls opened in 1867. But the staple Devonshire teas and requisite plum pudding that characterized the region's cuisine of old have been replaced by fluffy ricotta hotcakes drizzled with rich orange curd.

Among the handful of gastronomic trailblazers is Darleys, the restaurant at the country-house hotel Lilianfels, in Katoomba. Chef Hugh Whitehouse's menu features local ingredients, with an emphasis on game; the quail sausage and rabbit tortellini are highlights. After dinner, stop by the bar, which does killer martinis and authentic Peruvian pisco sours.

At Solitary Restaurant in the town of Leura, the French-leaning menu of

The dining room at Solitary restaurant, overlooking Jamison Valley, left. Below: Afternoon tea served fireside at Lilianfels, at Echo Point in Katoomba. Opposite: The Three Sisters sandstone spires near Katoomba.

self-taught chef John Cross (a solicitor in a former life, who still dabbles in the law) is a revelation of earthly delights. It's served in an attractive room decorated in soothing caffè latte tones, with white-clothed tables and dark-stained bistro chairs. An amuse-bouche of creamy leek and potato soup is followed by a sea urchin soufflé that is light yet complex in flavor; it's like catching the evening mist on your tongue. The Thirlmere spatchcock with crisp skin and a tarragon custard (a dish made with poultry bred in the nearby Southern Highlands) is a wonderful reworking of a classic.

Drive along the orchard-lined Bells Line of Road (by far the most scenic route through the mountains) to the quieter northern side of the Blue Mountains National Park. In Bilpin, which is famous for its abundant supply of apples, you'll find the appropriately named Apple Bar. From his wood-fired oven

and grill, chef Michael Jaggard produces divine thin-crusted pizzas, pork loin with caramelized apples, and Chinese-style *char siu* pork ribs. The space's indoor/outdoor quality, as well as its pints of local lager Coopers, give it the relaxed feel of a country pub. Daily specials vary according to available produce. Expect anything from octopus braised with feta, olives, and wild oregano to pavlovas topped with a jumble of fresh figs from an area grower.

On the way back to Sydney, near Kurrajong, is Lochiel House, in an

1825 wood-and-sandstone cottage built by one of the area's first settlers, former convict Joseph Douglass. Owners Monique Maul and Anthony Milroy are members of the vast network of alumni who studied under master Sydney chef Neil Perry (she worked at Wockpool, he at Perry's flagship, Rockpool), a heritage evident in their superlative Chinese-style spanner crab omelette—featherlight, intensely flavored, and a textural delight. Asian and Mediterranean influences shine through in dishes such as delicately spiced curries that use regional pro-duce—foraged mushrooms, handpicked native hibiscus—from suppliers who are thanked on the menu. Like the staging inns of yesteryear, Lochiel House is an essential stop to, or from, the mountains. If nothing else, pop in and sample scones with jam and cream on the front veranda or in the pretty courtyard. +

For The Guide, see page 280.

DON'T MISS

Scenic World, Katoomba
Get a bird's-eye view of this World Heritage Site from the Scenic Skyway, Scenic Rail-way, or Scenic Cableway.

Mt. Tomah Botanic Garden, Bilpin A glorious spot; home to the rare Wollemi pine.

La Maison du Livre, Leura Antiques bookseller Claude-Henri Dani's treasure trove of old and rare books has provided fantastic finds since 1977.

SPIRITED
AWAY   **Melbourne's Animated Nightlife**

Outside Misty Place bar, a longtime Melbourne favorite, above left. Above right: Booths at Meyers Place, in the CBD. Opposite: Inside Misty Place.

MELBOURNE'S NIGHTLIFE SCENE delivers a sense of excitement, the promise that if you push the right scuffed and peeling door, you might be transported into an intimate space that makes you forget about the outside world. Over the past decade, there's been an explosion of secret places stamped with their owners' personalities. Closely linked to the city's creative community, these watering holes often host innovative street parties and local bands. Some of the best are hidden down graffiti-covered lanes or above abandoned warehouses.

The influx of bars started in 1994, when draconian drinking laws (forcing patrons to eat when they drank) were overturned to give the city's Crown Casino a leg up. This law ultimately didn't apply just to the casino; as a result, there are now nearly 200 bars in the Central Business District (CBD). Meyers Place was the second outpost after Crown to benefit from the new license. It's part coffee shop, part bar; a spot where friends can sip a drink and talk.

Many of the new establishments reference other cultures in their designs and their cocktail lists. One of the more exotic is Manchuria, where the look is Chinese-antique: brightly colored silk cushions, and moody lighting. What's most impressive are the inventive drinks, such as the Ramos Fizz, made with gin, orange-blossom water, and a foamy egg-white top. A second

Street art along a small lane in Melbourne's Central Business District, above left. Above right: A lounge area at Double Happiness bar.

Asian-inspired bar, Double Happiness, takes a political turn: enthusiastic Communists raise their fists from propaganda posters on the walls, and cocktails have names like the Long March.

Nearby, the Greek-themed Baraki Upo Mezethes forgoes a cocktail list in favor of beer, but bartender Andrew Morley is a whiz at whipping up anything you want on the fly. Ask him for a Happy Ending—a spicy, sour concoction with vodka, coriander, and *piri-piri* (chile) sauce. Then there's

Robot, a shrine to Japanese pop culture. The two-story space is a top-notch sushi bar by day, and an equally popular cocktail spot at night. (On Tuesdays, it has free screenings of anime.)

For faded 1950's glamour, stop by Tony Starr's Kitten Club, with its diner-style interior; the upstairs Galaxy Lounge is a showcase for jazz. Another bar referencing the old guard is Gin Palace, which has an opium-den feel, with large rococo chairs and excellent martinis, like the Chicago 1951, a mix of gin, Cointreau, and vermouth.

Even amid all the new bars, certain veterans are still worth a visit. Misty Place looks like a work of art, with cutout paper lampshades, amber lights, and a gorgeous crowd to match. ✦

For The Guide, see page 280.

CALL OF THE WILD

**A Sailing Tour of
Tasmania's Bruny Island**

BRUNY ISLAND LIES BELOW TASMANIA'S southeast coast, the last stop before Antarctica. Little has changed here since Jacques-Julien Houtou de Labillardière, a French botanist, described the spectacular cliffs in 1793 as "reddish sandstone, disposed in parallel strata perpendicular to the horizon." The isolated location has left the island with a rich history of discovery that is being shaped by a group of entrepreneurs who are making Bruny a new frontier for outdoor adventure.

See the coast with Rob Pennicott of Bruny Island Charters. As his three-engine sightseeing boat navigates chasms surrounded by impressive rock formations, schools of dolphins dance through the water. The main beach, Adventure Bay, is pristine and empty. Pennicott says he was drawn here by "the wilderness, wildlife, and lack of people—all that is lacking in the world now." +

For The Guide, see page 281.

Exploring the caves and chasms of Tasmania's Bruny Island, with Bruny Island Charters.

KIWI WINE COUNTRY

New Zealand's Waiheke Island

IN THE 1970'S, WHEN VINTNERS KIM AND JEANETTE GOLDWATER arrived on Waiheke Island, a 35-minute ferry ride from Auckland, the place was home to little more than a few retirees. "The biggest industry was welfare," Kim says.

The couple planted their first vines on a slope overlooking Putiki Bay. Today, the Goldwater Estate has become one of New Zealand's leading red-wine producers, and the island itself has grown into a posh playground: mega-yachts bob in the aquamarine waters, and a growing number of millionaires' mansions dot the undulating landscape of green hills, volcanic ridges, and rain forests.

With hot, dry summers, free-draining soils, and a maritime influence, the conditions here are ideal for boutique wineries.

The hills of the Te Whau peninsula, on New Zealand's Waiheke Island.

In wine-speak, Waiheke has more "growing degree" days than Bordeaux, Napa, Coonawarra, and Hawke's Bay—the other regions that produce some of the world's great Cabernet blends. One enthusiastic commentator was even moved to declare the climate "more like Bordeaux than Bordeaux."

Another part of Waiheke's appeal: visitors can traverse the small island in just 25 minutes, from sparsely populated Waiheke to Te Matuku Bay, where David Evans-Gander runs the unpretentious Passage Rock Wines. His Forte is one of Waiheke's most distinguished reds. After a tasting, head to the café, at the end of a row of vines, for wood-fired pizza.

New Zealand's answer to Château Margaux is Stonyridge Larose, produced by laid-back yachtsman Stephen White. After working in vineyards in California and Italy, the fifth-generation Aucklander identified Waiheke Island as the place to make his cult Cabernet blend, packed with spicy, minty fruit flavors. Set amid fields of lavender and mature olive trees halfway between Onetangi Beach and Putiki Bay, the Stonyridge vineyard is an attractive place, but it isn't the best place to sample or

An entrance to the Stonyridge vineyard, in the center of Waiheke Island, above. Top left: A rack of wines at the Te Whau vineyard, on the Te Whau peninsula. Bottom left: In front of the Waiheke Wine Centre, in Oneroa.

T+L Tip

Fullers Ferries runs regular passenger services from Auckland to Waiheke, 35 minutes away; SeaLink's car ferry takes 45 minutes.

purchase Larose. A better option is the Waiheke Wine Centre, in Oneroa—a must for any wine aficionado. The shop stocks a range of bottles, and they're cheaper here than at the winery.

Ironically, the ideal spot to try a few back vintages of Larose is at another vineyard, Te Whau. Owner Tony Forsyth is one of New Zealand's leading collectors, and for the past 30 years he has been building an impressive cellar, available at the property's Le Corbusier–influenced restaurant. The views from the striking space are as good as the grapes: the vine-covered hillside falls away steeply toward the water below, clearing the way for a panoramic view across the gulf to the Auckland skyline. +

For The Guide, see page 281.

TROPICAL BOUNTY

The Private-Island Paradise of Fiji

Ugaga Island, home to the Royal Davui resort.

IN MANY WAYS, FIJI IS LIKE A SNAPSHOT OF HAWAII before the high-rises. The sugarcane republic has fewer than 1 million residents and a single two-lane highway. For travelers who harbor South Seas fantasies fueled by old Humphrey Bogart films, crossing the International Date Line to reach the archipelago of 322 islands has its payoff: it's one of the last untrammeled places on earth, where steamer ferries still ply the straits and barefoot bush pilots land on grass strips to deliver guitar strings and watermelons.

The 2,200-acre Wakaya Island has been transformed into a quiet paradise by David Gilmour, the man who founded FIJI Water. Stay in one of the 10 cinnabar-red bungalows, and snorkel on the shoreline in the company of the angelfish and yellow tang, who noodle around chunks of coral.

On Ugaga Island, an eight-acre gumdrop, the Royal Davui resort's 16 mahogany villas cling to cliffs overlooking a marine sanctuary and a shallow reef that ripples turquoise and silver at dusk.

Eco-conscious travelers will gravitate toward Nukubati Island, which runs on solar power. Rainwater is collected in cisterns; women from nearby villages weave floor mats for the plantation-style lodge. Guests reach the seven-room resort by seaplane, which glides to a stop in a lagoon. It's a new perception of far, far away. ✦

For The Guide, see page 281.

→ THE GUIDE

Here you'll find a complete directory of the hotels, restaurants, shops, and more featured in the preceding pages.

UNITED STATES + CANADA

NANTUCKET, MA

WHERE TO STAY
Sherburne Inn Simple bed-and-breakfast in the center of town. 10 Gay St.; 508/228-4425; sherburneinn.com; doubles from $$. **The Wauwinet** The island's exclusive, white-fenced luxury resort. 120 Wauwinet Rd.; 800/426-8718 or 508/228-0145; wauwinet.com; doubles from $$$$.
WHERE TO EAT
Black-Eyed Susan's Nantucket's best breakfast.10 India St.; 508/325-0308; breakfast for two ❚❚. **Even Keel Café** Delicious French toast. 40 Main St.; 508/228-1979; brunch for two ❚.
WHERE TO SHOP
Murray's Toggery Shop Traditional Nantucket attire. 62 Main St.; 508/228-0437. **Peter Beaton Hat Studio** Hats and totes made from braided leghorn straw. 16½ Federal St.; 508/228-8456.
WHAT TO DO
Young's Bicycle Shop Rentals from the oldest bike shop on the island. 6 Broad St.; 508/228-1151.

BOSTON

WHERE TO STAY
XV Beacon Hotel Early-20th-century Beaux-Arts building. 15 Beacon St.; 877/982-3226 or 617/670-1500; xvbeacon.com; doubles from $$$.
WHAT TO DO
Institute of Contemporary Art Vast collection, plus on-site music, dance, and theater performances. 100 Northern Ave.; 617/478-3100; icaboston.org.

NEW CANAAN, CT

WHERE TO STAY
Roger Sherman Inn Cozy 18th-century Colonial inn. 195 Oenoke Ridge; 203/966-4541; rogershermaninn.com; doubles from $$.
WHAT TO DO
Glass House Philip Johnson's iconic former residence, now open for tours. 199 Elm St.; 203/966-8167; philipjohnsonglasshouse.org.

BURLINGTON, VT

WHERE TO STAY
Inn at Essex 10 miles from downtown, with handy kitchenettes. 70 Essex Way, Essex Junction; 800/727-4295 or 802/878-1100; innatessex.com; doubles from $$. **Wyndham Burlington** 257-room hotel with indoor pool. 60 Battery St.; 800/996-3426 or 802/658-6500; wyndham.com; doubles from $$.
WHERE TO EAT
Al's French Frys Burgers with the works. 1251 Williston Rd., South Burlington; 802/862-9203; lunch for two ❚. **Penny Cluse Café** Popular breakfast joint with gingerbread pancakes and freshly squeezed tangerine juice. 169 Cherry St.; 802/651-8834; breakfast for two ❚.
WHAT TO DO
Flynn Center for Performing Arts Everything from hip-hop jams to Russian ballet. 153 Main St.; 802/863-5966; flynncenter.org. **Horticultural Research Center** 97-acre farm, also known as Hort Farm, with more than 700 kinds of trees. 65 Green Mountain Dr., South Burlington; 802/658-9166. **Paul Miller Research Complex** Daily dairy cow milkings. 500 Spear St.; no phone. **Perkins Geology Museum** Hands-on exhibits include rock identification and microscopic examination. 180 Colchester Ave.; 802/656-8694; uvm.edu.

NEW YORK CITY

WHERE TO STAY
Gramercy Park Hotel Julian Schnabel–designed, velvet-draped interiors. 2 Lexington Ave.; 877/898-3200 or 212/920-3300; gramercyparkhotel.com; doubles from $$$. **Hotel QT** Hip on a budget. 125 W. 45th St.; 212/354-2323; hotelqt.com; $$. **Mandarin Oriental New York** Asian-inspired. 80 Columbus Circle; 800/526-6566 or 212/805-8800; mandarinoriental.com; doubles from $$$$.
WHERE TO EAT
Clinton St. Baking Co. & Restaurant Neighborhood brunch spot, with standout

DINING   under $25 → ❚ $25-$74 → ❚❚ $75-$149 → ❚❚❚ $150-$299 → ❚❚❚❚ $300 + up → ❚❚❚❚❚

muffins and buttermilk biscuits. 4 Clinton St.; 646/602-6263; breakfast for two 🍴🍴. **Degustation** 16-seat counter serving tapas-scaled triumphs. 239 E. Fifth St.; 212/979-1012; dinner for two 🍴🍴. **Doughnut Plant** Oversize doughnuts with all-natural, fresh-fruit glazes. 379 Grand St.; 212/505-3700. **Falai** Euro-chic neighborhood trattoria. 68 Clinton St.; 212/253-1960; dinner for two 🍴🍴🍴. **L'Atelier de Joël Robuchon** Manhattan branch of the French chef's galaxy of haute dining bars. 57 E. 57th St.; 212/350-6658; dinner for two 🍴🍴🍴🍴. **Momofuku** Manhattan's zeitgeist bar-restaurant, famous for ramen. 163 First Ave.; 212/475-7899; dinner for two 🍴🍴🍴. **Per Se** Thomas Keller's perfect, farm-based dishes. Time Warner Center, 10 Columbus Circle, 4th floor; 212/823-9335; dinner for two 🍴🍴🍴🍴. **Spotted Pig** Michelin-starred gastropub. 314 W. 11th St.; 212/620-0393; lunch for two 🍴🍴. **Una Pizza Napoletana** Elevated pies. 349 E. 12th St.; 212/477-9950; dinner for two 🍴🍴.

WHERE TO SHOP

Atmos Outpost of a Tokyo sneaker store, with exclusive styles. 203 W. 125th St.; 212/666-2242. **Denim Library** 35 brands of jeans for men and women. 2326 Seventh Ave.; 212/281-2380. **Everything Must Go** Skate shop, with hard-to-find labels. 2281 First Ave.; 212/722-8203. **Montgomery** Small boutique with chic women's pieces, plus jewelry. 2312 Seventh Ave.; 212/690-2166. **N** 4,000 square feet of clothing, baubles, and more. 114 W. 116th St.; 212/961-1036.

WASHINGTON, D.C.

WHERE TO STAY

Hotel Helix Pucci-inspired 178-room kitsch palace; walls are covered in green lizard-skin wallpaper or white leather. 1430 Rhode Island Ave. NW; 866/508-0658 or 202/462-9001; hotelhelix.com; doubles from **$**. **Hotel Rouge** High style meets major attitude, with zebra-print robes and mini-bars stocked with Johnny Walker Red. 1315 16th St. NW; 800/368-5689 or 202/232-8000; rougehotel.com; doubles from **$$$**. **Willard InterContinental** Opulent 1901 Beaux-Arts icon, a short stroll from the Mall. 1401 Pennsylvania Avenue NW; 888/424-6835 or 202/628-9100; intercontinental.com; doubles from **$$$**.

WHERE TO EAT

Café Saint-Ex Run by a local-farm champion, with fried-green-tomato BLT's. 1847 14th St. NW; 202/265-7839; dinner for two 🍴🍴.

WHERE TO SHOP

Carbon Mod Chelsea boots and wingtips for men. 2643 Connecticut Ave. NW; 202/232-6645. **Muléh** Contemporary Asian furniture mixed with cutting-edge fashion. 1831 14th St. NW; 202/667-3440. **Nana** Airy second-floor atelier with affordable clothing and accessories from up-and-coming designers. 1528 U St. NW; 202/667-6955. **Wild Women Wear Red** Sexy yet practical shoes from labels like Camper and Lisa Nading. 1512 U St. NW; 202/387-5700.

WHAT TO DO

Irvine Contemporary Well-known early- and mid-career artists. 1412 14th St. NW; 202/332-8767; irvinecontemporary.com. **Nevin Kelly Gallery** Displays works from the Old and New Worlds. 1517 U St. NW; 202/232-3464; nevinkellygallery.com. **Project 4** Local talent in shows organized by guest curators. 903 U St. NW; 202/232-4340; project4gallery.com.

NIGHTLIFE

Gate 54 Lounge below Café Saint-Ex, with nightly DJ's. 1847 14th St. NW; 202/265-7839. **HR-57** Jazz club that hosts the city's best jam sessions on Wednesdays and Thursdays. 1610 14th St. NW; 202/667-3700.

ATLANTA

WHERE TO STAY

Four Seasons Hotel Contemporary midtown tower. 75 14th St.; 800/819-5053 or 404/881-9898; fourseasons.com; doubles from **$$$**. **Indigo** InterContinental Hotels' affordable boutique flagship. 683 Peachtree St.; 877/846-3446 or 800/465-4329; hotelindigo.com; doubles from **$**.

WHERE TO EAT

Krogbar Pocket-size wine bar, with a log-cabin feel. 112 Krog St.; 404/524-1618; dinner for two 🍴. **Lobby at Twelve** New American cooking in a loftlike setting. 361 17th St.; 404/961-7370; dinner for two 🍴🍴. **Piebar** Mod pizza restaurant, with an atomic-age design. 2160 Monroe Dr.; 404/815-1605; dinner for two 🍴🍴. **Quinones** 36-seat salon below the popular restaurant Bacchanalia. 1198 Howell Mill Rd.; 404/365-0410; dinner for two 🍴🍴🍴🍴. **Rolling Bones** A cheery barbecue joint with a retro feel. 377 Edgewood Ave.; 404/222-2324; dinner for two 🍴🍴. **Table 1280** Ambitious, well-executed American brasserie food and soaring, light-drenched rooms, in the Woodruff Arts Center. 1280 Peachtree St.; 404/897-1280; dinner for two 🍴🍴🍴.

MIAMI

WHERE TO STAY

Delano Ian Schrager's celebrity favorite. 1685 Collins Ave., Miami Beach; 800/697-1791 or 305/672-2000; delano-hotel.com; doubles from **$$$**. **Shore Club** Art Deco hotel with a major social scene. 1901 Collins Ave., Miami Beach; 800/697-1791 or 305/695-3100; shoreclub.com; doubles from **$$$**.

WHAT TO DO

Art Basel Miami Beach Annual 5-day contemporary art fair with exhibits and parties throughout the city. 300 W 41st St., Miami Beach; 305/674-1292; artbaselmiamibeach.com.

AUSTIN, TX

WHERE TO STAY

Hotel San José Renovated motel, with concrete floors covered in cowhide rugs. 1316 S. Congress Ave.; 800/574-8897 or 512/444-7322; sanjosehotel.com; doubles from **$$**.

WHERE TO EAT

Jo's Funky neighborhood

café. 1300 S. Congress Ave.; 512/444-3800; breakfast for two ❘. **P & K Grocery** Corner store with pies and gourmet boxed lunches. 915 W. Mary St.; 512/326-3133; lunch for two ❘.

WHERE TO SHOP

By George Women's clothing boutique. 1400 S. Congress Ave.; 512/441-8600. **Uncommon Objects** Vast antiques and ephemera store. 1512 S. Congress Ave.; 512/442-4000.

NIGHTLIFE

Continental Club Live music venue with retro vibe. 1315 S. Congress Ave.; 512/441-2444.

OHIO

WHERE TO STAY

The Cincinnatian Cincinnati's grandest hotel, with fireplaces and soaking tubs. 601 Vine St., Cincinnati; 800/942-9000 or 513/381-3000; cincinnatianhotel. com; doubles from **$$**. **Park Inn** Centrally located tower near the Maumee River. 101 N. Summit St., Toledo; 888/201-1801 or 419/241-3000; parkinn.com; doubles from **$**.

WHAT TO DO

Contemporary Arts Center New Zaha Hadid–designed building. 44 E. Sixth St., Cincinnati; 513/345-8400; contemporaryartscenter. org. **Glass Pavilion, Toledo Museum of Art** The work of Japanese firm SANAA, housing gallery space and glassmaking studios. 2445 Monroe St., Toledo; 419/255-8000; toledomuseum.org.

WISCONSIN

WHERE TO STAY

Hotel Metro Small Art Deco–style property with bamboo floors, Jacuzzis, and in-room CD players. 411 E. Mason St., Milwaukee; 877/638-7620 or 414/272-1937; hotelmetro. com; doubles from **$$**.

WHAT TO DO

Milwaukee Art Museum Santiago Calatrava revamped the entrance hall of the 1950's Eero Saarinen building. 700 N. Art Museum Dr., Milwaukee; 414/224-3200; mam.org.

MINNESOTA

WHERE TO STAY

Chambers Minneapolis Minimalist hotel packed with maximalist art. 901 Hennepin Ave., Minneapolis; 877/767-6990 or 612/767-6900; chambers minneapolis.com; doubles from **$$$**.

WHAT TO DO

Walker Art Center Contemporary art in a space by architects Herzog & de Meuron. 1750 Hennepin Ave., Minneapolis; 612/375-7600; walkerart.org.

IOWA

WHERE TO STAY

Alexis Park Inn Quirky all-suite aviation-themed hotel. 1165 S. Riverside Dr., Iowa City; 888/925-3947 or 319/337-8665; alexisparkinn.com; doubles from **$**. **Suites of 800 Locust** Renovated 5-story 1912 boutique property downtown. 800 Locust St., Des Moines; 800/320-2580

or 515/288-5800; 800locust. com; doubles from **$$**.

WHAT TO DO

Des Moines Public Library Copper-clad building. 100 Grand Ave.; 515/283-4152; pldminfo.org. **School of Art and Art History** Modernist steel structure cantilevered over a pond. 150 Art Building West, 141 North Riverside Dr., University of Iowa, Iowa City; 319/335-1771; art.uiowa.edu.

CHICAGO

WHERE TO STAY

Hotel Blake Modern amenities like iPod docking stations; the South Loop's newest arrival. 500 S. Dearborn St.; 312/986-1234; hotelblake.com; doubles from **$$$**. **Peninsula Chicago** Sleek tower with stylish interiors and a rooftop spa. 108 East Superior St.; 866/288-8889 or 312/337-2888; peninsula. com; doubles from **$$$**.

WHERE TO EAT

Alinea Experimental tasting menus. 1723 N. Halstead St.; 312/867-0110; dinner for two ❘❘❘❘. **Custom House** Top-notch steaks. 500 S. Dearborn St.; 312/523-0200; dinner for two ❘❘❘. **Quartino** Old-world Italian in small plates. 626 N. State St.; 312/698-5000; dinner for two ❘❘. **Schwa** Tiny BYOB spot. 1466 N. Ashland Ave.; 773/252-1466; dinner for two ❘❘❘.

BRECKENRIDGE, CO

WHERE TO STAY

Four Peaks Inn 7-room historic B&B. 407 S. Ridge St.;

970/453-3813; fourpeaks inn.com; doubles from **$**.

WHERE TO EAT

Quandary Grille American fare in a rustic atmosphere. 505 Main St.; 970/547-5969; dinner for two ❘❘. **South Ridge Seafood Grill** Casual seafood restaurant and bar. 215 S. Ridge St.; 970/547-0063; dinner for two ❘❘.

WHERE TO SHOP

Colorado Freeride Complete gear for the slopes. 114 North Main St.; 970/453-0995.

WYOMING

WHERE TO STAY

Best Western Plaza Hotel Open-air mineral pool. 116 E. Park St., Hot Springs State Park, Thermopolis; 888/919-9009 or 307/864-2939; bestwestern.com; doubles from **$**. **Occidental Hotel** The oldest in Wyoming. 10 N. Main St., Buffalo; 307/684-0451; occidentalwyoming.com; doubles from **$**.

WHERE TO EAT

Buffalo Bill's Irma Hotel Restaurant & Saloon Best for lunch or drinks. 1192 Sheridan Ave., Cody; 307/587-4221; lunch for two ❘❘. **Elk Horn Bar & Grill** Authentic spot, with hundreds of boots hanging from the ceiling. 916 State St., Meeteetse; 307/868-9245; dinner for two ❘❘. **Proud Cut Saloon & Bar** Cowboy cuisine. 1227 Sheridan Ave., Cody; 307/527-6905; dinner for two ❘❘. **Wyoming's Rib & Chop House** At the Sheridan Inn. 856 N. Broadway St., Sheridan; 307/673-4700; dinner for two ❘❘.

WHAT TO DO

Cody Nite Rodeo Nightly

shows from the beginning of June through August. Yellowstone Ave., Cody; 307/587-5155. **Cowboy Bar** Butch Cassidy was arrested here in 1894. 1936 State St., Meeteetse; 307/868-2585. **Old Trail Town** 25 historic buildings, reconstructed on the outskirts of town. 1831 Demaris Dr., Cody; 307/587-5302. **Sheridan Inn** Historic museum displays where Buffalo Bill Cody auditioned acts for his Wild West shows; reopening as a hotel this year. 856 Broadway St., Sheridan; 307/673-4700; sheridaninn. com. **Star Plunge** Water park with hot-mineral pools, a vapor cave, and massage therapy. 115 Big Springs Drive, Hot Springs State Park, Thermopolis; 307/864-3771. **State Bath House** Glass-enclosed hot soaking pool. Hot Springs State Park, Thermopolis; 307/864-2176.

UTAH

WHERE TO STAY
Red Mountain Spa Adventure spa in desert setting. 1275 E. Red Mountain Circle, Ivins; 800/407-3002 or 435/673-4905; redmountainspa.com; doubles from **$$**, including all meals.

LAS VEGAS

WHERE TO STAY
Venetian Resort & Casino Colossal Italianate fantasy with faux Grand Canal. 3355 Las Vegas Blvd. S.; 877/883-6423 or 702/414-1000; doubles from **$$**. **Wynn Las Vegas** Sophisticated hotel on the Strip, behind a

man-made mountain. 3131 Las Vegas Blvd. S.; 888/320-9966 or 702/770-7000; wynnlasvegas.com; doubles from **$$$**.
WHERE TO EAT
Buffet at TI One of the new breed of "hip buffets." Treasure Island, 3300 Las Vegas Blvd. S.; 702/894-7111; dinner for two ⫙.
NIGHTLIFE
Mix Lounge Curvy black-leather banquettes and views of the Strip from the 64th floor. 3950 Las Vegas Blvd. S.; 877/632-7800 or 702/632-7777. **Peppermill's Fireside Lounge** 1970's spot with cocktail waitresses in long black gowns, velour booths, and a fire pit. 2985 Las Vegas Blvd S.; 702/735-4177. **Pure** One of the city's hottest clubs. Inside Caesars Palace, 3570 Las Vegas Blvd. S.; 702/731-7873.

ANAHEIM, CA

WHERE TO STAY
Disney's Grand Californian Hotel & Spa Craftsman-style lodge adjacent to Downtown Disney. 714/635-2300; disneyland. com; doubles from **$$$**. **Disneyland Hotel** Big pools, and nearly as close to the park as the Grand Californian (but with fewer frills). 714/778-6600; disneyland. com; doubles from **$$**.

LOS ANGELES

WHERE TO STAY
Chamberlain West Hollywood 4 stories full of whimsically ornate furniture. 1000 Westmount Dr., West Hollywood; 800/201-9637 or 310/657-7400;

chamberlainwesthollywood. com; doubles from **$$**. **Sunset Tower Hotel** The historic Sunset hotel, returned to its original Hollywood glamour. 8358 Sunset Blvd., West Hollywood; 800/225-2637 or 323/654-7100; sunsettowerhotel. com; doubles from **$$$$**.
WHERE TO SHOP
Delia Lesser-known European designers. 8438 Melrose Place; 323/658-8685. **Diane von Furstenberg** Find the wrap-dress classic, plus a line of jewelry created in collaboration with H.Stern. 8407 Melrose Ave.; 323/951-1947. **Duncan Quinn** Savile Row tailoring with a rock 'n' roll edge. 8380 Melrose Ave.; 323/782-9205. **Marc by Marc Jacobs** Jacobs's less-pricey diffusion label. 8410 Melrose Ave.; 323/653-0100. **Me & Ro** Buddhist-inspired jewelry. 8405 Melrose Place; 323/782-1071. **Paul Smith** The British designer's 5,000-square-foot L.A. flagship. 8221 Melrose Ave.; 323/951-4800. **Suzanne Felsen** Hand-selected modern gems. 8332 Melrose Ave.; 323/653-5400. **RetroSpecs & Co.** More than 3,000 vintage eyeglass-frame designs. 8458 Melrose Place; 323/951-0215. **Temperley London** British design house known for beading, embroidery, and feminine prints. 8452 Melrose Place; 323/782-8000.

MALIBU, CA

WHERE TO STAY
Malibu Beach Inn 47 rooms with private balconies, all within earshot of the surf.

22878 Pacific Coast Hwy.; 800/462-5428 or 310/456-6444; malibubeachinn.com; doubles from **$$$**.
WHAT TO DO
Getty Villa Classical-arts museum. 17985 Pacific Coast Hwy.; 310/440-7300; getty.edu.

HEALDSBURG, CA

WHERE TO STAY
Hotel Healdsburg Polished, tranquil hotel, done up in an earthy palette. 25 Matheson St.; 800/889-7188 or 707/431-2800; hotelhealdsburg. com; doubles from **$$$**. **Les Mars Hotel** Antiques from the 17th and 18th centuries in an inn patterned after a French château. 27 North St.; 877/431-1700 or 707/433-4211; lesmarshotel.com; doubles from **$$$**.
WHERE TO EAT
Barndiva Late-night meals and creative cocktails. 231 Center St.; 707/431-0100; dinner for two ⫙⫙. **Cyrus** Intuitive service and exquisite dishes by rising chef Douglas Keane. 29 North St.; 707/433-3311; dinner for two ⫙⫙⫙. **Dry Creek Kitchen** A Sonoma-only wine menu and local farm-sourced ingredients under chef Charlie Palmer. 317 Healdsburg Ave.; 707/431-0330; dinner for two ⫙⫙.
WHERE TO SHOP
M Clothing Women's labels, including Theory, Nanette Lepore, and Scoop. 381 Healdsburg Ave.; 707/431-8738. **Myra Hoefer Design** French-influenced interior design shop. 309 Healdsburg Ave.; 707/433-7837.
WHAT TO DO
Thumbprint Cellars Small

bottlings of micro-wines. 36 North St.; 707/433-2393. **Toad Hollow** Known for its no-oak Chardonnays. 409A Healdsburg Ave.; 707/431-8667.

HAWAII

WHERE TO STAY
Volcano House Rustic 1846 lodge on the edge of Kilauea Crater. Hawaii Volcanoes National Park; 808/967-7321; volcano househotel.com; doubles from **$**. **Volcano Rainforest Retreat** 4 cottages with wood beams, large skylights, and Japanese-style soaking tubs. 11–3832 12th St.; 800/550-8696 or 808/985-8696; volcanoretreat. com; doubles from **$**.
WHAT TO DO
Hawaii Volcanoes National Park Tour lava fields surrounding the world's most active volcano. 1 Crater Rim Dr., Big Island; 808/985-6000; nps.gov. **Tropical Helicopters** Aerial tours of Kilauea volcano. 808/961-6810; tropicalhelicopters.com.

NOVA SCOTIA

WHERE TO STAY
Boscawen Inn 1888 Victorian mansion. 150 Cumberland St., Lunenburg; 800/354-5009 or 902/634-3325; boscawen.ca; doubles from **$**. **Inn at Bay Fortune** Former artist's retreat on 46 grassy acres on the bay. Rte. 310, Bay Fortune; 888/687-3745 or 902/687-3745; innatbayfortune.com; doubles from **$$**.
WHERE TO EAT
Fleur de Sel Traditional French cuisine. 53 Mon-

tague St., Lunenburg; 902/640-2121; dinner for two ¶¶¶. **Rusty Anchor** Locally caught seafood. 23197 Cabot Trail Rd., Pleasant Bay; 902/224-1313; dinner for two ¶¶.
WHERE TO SHOP
Co-op Artisanale Hooked rugs, wall hangings, and doilies from 75 area artists. 15067 Cabot Trail Rd., Chéticamp; 902/224-2170. **Leather Works** Hand-sewn belts, wallets, and bags. 45808 Cabot Trail Rd., Indian Brook; 902/929-2414. **Myles from Nowhere** Funky 2-story shack filled with ephemera. 7889 Cabot Trail Rd., Margaree Forks; 902/248-2336.
WHAT TO DO
Museum of Hooked Rugs & Home Life Displays of hooked rugs. 15584 Cabot Trail Rd., Chéticamp; 902/224-2642; lestrois pignons.com. **Nova Scotia Folk Art Festival** Held first Sunday in August. Green St. & Victoria Rd., Lunenburg; 902/634-8744.

QUEBEC CITY

WHERE TO STAY
Auberge St.-Antoine Old World details. 10 Rue St.-Antoine; 888/692-2211 or 418/692-2211; saint-antoine.com; doubles from **$$**.
WHERE TO EAT
L'Astral Rotating rooftop restaurant. 1225 Cours du Général de Montcalm; 418/647-2222; dinner for two ¶¶. **Le Café St.-Malo** Rustic French food. 75 Rue St.-Paul; 418/692-2004; dinner for two ¶¶.

WHAT TO DO
Carnaval de Quebec 17-day winter festival. 290 Rue Joly; 418/626-3716; carnaval.qc.ca. **Patinoire de la Place d'Youville** Skating rink, set in a centrally located square. Place d'Youville; 418/641-6256.

TORONTO

WHERE TO STAY
The Drake A hub of design, art, and music. 1150 Queen St. W.; 800/553-7253 or 416/531-5042; thedrakehotel.ca; doubles from **$$**.
WHERE TO EAT
Bymark Refined comfort food. 66 Wellington St.; 416/777-1144; dinner for two ¶¶¶. **Czehoski** Experimental cuisine, in a former butcher shop. 678 Queen St. W.; 416/366-6787; dinner for two ¶¶. **Jamie Kennedy Wine Bar** Extensive wine cellar and small plates. 9 Church St.; 416/362-1957; dinner for two ¶¶¶.
WHERE TO SHOP
Commute Home Modern furnishings. 819 Queen St. W.; 416/861-0521. **Delphic** Acne Jeans and handbags by supermodel Alek Wek. 706 Queen St. W.; 416/603-3334.
WHAT TO DO
Art Gallery of Ontario Collection spanning 19 centuries; a new Frank Gehry expansion is set to open this year. 317 Dundas St. W.; 416/979-6648; ago. net. **Camera** Screening room owned by filmmaker Atom Egoyan. 1028 Queen St. W.; 416/530-0011. **Four Seasons Centre for the Performing Arts** Home of the Canadian Opera

Company and the National Ballet. 145 Queen St. W.; 416/363-6671; fourseasonscentre.ca. **Ontario College of Art & Design** New addition by Will Alsop is causing a stir. 100 McCaul St.; 416/977-6000; ocad.on.ca. **Royal Ontario Museum** Steel-and-glass expansion designed by Daniel Libeskind. 100 Queen's Park; 416/586-8000; rom. on.ca.

BRITISH COLUMBIA

WHERE TO STAY
Hotel Eldorado Lakeside lodge with claw-foot bathtubs and fireplaces. 500 Cook Rd., Kelowna; 866/608-7500 or 250/763-7500; eldoradokelowna. com; doubles from **$$**.
WHAT TO DO
Carmelis Goat Cheese Artisan Known for its sweet, nutty parmesan and raw-milk chèvre. 170 Timberline Rd., Kelowna; 250/470-0341. **CedarCreek** Family-run hillside winery with a California-trained winemaker. 5445 Lakeshore Rd., Kelowna; 250/764-8866. **Mission Hill Family Estate** 900-acre vineyard. 1730 Mission Hill Rd., Westbank; 250/768-6448. **Nk'Mip Cellars** Aboriginal-owned and -operated winery, with native art and artifacts on display. 1400 Rancher Creek Rd., Osoyoos; 250/495-2985. **Quails' Gate Estate Winery** Pinot Noir and Chardonnay are the specialties. 3303 Boucherie Rd., Kelowna; 250/769-4451.

Harbour
Island

Dominican
Republic

Grand
Cayman

St. John

British Virgin
Islands

**CARIBBEAN +
THE BAHAMAS**

St. Lucia

CARIBBEAN +
THE BAHAMAS

ST. LUCIA

WHERE TO STAY

Cap Maison Apartment-style boutique hotel; opening March 2008. Smugglers Cove Drive, Cap Estate; 758/450-8847; capmaison. com; doubles from **$$$**. **Cotton Bay Village** Exclusive beachfront resort. Cas-en-Bas, Castries; 800/544-2883 or 758/457-7871; cottonbay village.com; doubles from **$$$**. **Discovery at Marigot Bay** Village-style resort, with marina. Marigot; 866/440-6600 or 758/458-5300; discoverystlucia.com; doubles from **$$$**. **The Landings** Lavish new property from RockResorts; opening December 2007. Rodney Bay; 888-367-7625; rockresorts.com; doubles from **$$$**, all inclusive.

CARIBBEAN CRUISE

Freedom of the Seas The world's biggest cruise ship. 800/327-6700; royal caribbean.com; from $849 per person for a 7-night cruise.

ST. JOHN

WHERE TO STAY

Maho Bay Camps Tented cabins. Maho Bay; 800/392-9004 or 340/715-0501; maho.org; doubles from **$**. **Concordia Eco-Tents** Environmentally friendly resort. Maho Bay; 800/392-9004 or 340/715-0501; maho.org; doubles from **$$**.

BRITISH VIRGIN ISLANDS

WHERE TO STAY

Biras Creek Resort Secluded retreat. Berchers Bay, Virgin Gorda; 800/223-1100 or 284/494-3555; biras.com; doubles from **$$$$**. **Bitter End Yacht Club** Good for sailors. North Sound, Virgin Gorda; 800/872-2392 or 312/506-6205; beyc.com; villas from **$$$**. **Little Dix Bay, A Rosewood Resort** Recently redone legend. Little Dix Bay, Virgin Gorda; 888/767-3966 or 284/495-5555; littledixbay.com; doubles from **$$$$**. **Peter Island** Private-island resort. Peter Island; 800/346-4451 or 284/495-2000; peterisland. com; doubles from **$$$$**. **Sugar Mill Hotel** Small inn with gourmet restaurant. Little Apple Bay, Tortola; 800/462-8834 or 284/495-4355; sugarmillhotel.com; doubles from **$$$**.

WHERE TO EAT

The Dove Global menu in a sweet Caribbean cottage. 67 Main St., Road Town, Tortola; 284/494-0313; dinner for two 🍴🍴🍴

WHAT TO DO

Aragorn's Studio Arts center with handmade regional products for sale. Trellis Bay, Tortola; 284/495-1849; aragornsstudio.com.

DOMINICAN REPUBLIC

WHERE TO STAY

Sofitel Nicolas de Ovando Built in 1502. Calle Las Damas, Santo Domingo; 800/763-4835 or 809/685-9955; sofitel.com; doubles from **$$$**.

WHERE TO EAT

Mesón d'Bari Spanish-Dominican menu. 302 Hostos St., Santo Domingo; 809/687-4091; dinner for two 🍴🍴

WHAT TO DO

Alcázar de Colón Old palace. Plaza de España, Santo Domingo; 809/686-8657. **Catedral Primada de América** The Western Hemisphere's first church. Arzobispo Meriño St. and Arzobispo Nouel St., Santo Domingo; no phone. **Fortaleza Ozama** Ancient fort, off Calle de las Damas, Santo Domingo. **Hospital San Nicolas de Bari** Ancient ruins. Calle Hostos, Santo Domingo; no phone.

GRAND CAYMAN

WHERE TO STAY

Ritz-Carlton, Grand Cayman Golf, high-end restaurants. Seven Mile Beach; 800/241-3333 or 345/943-9000; ritzcarlton.com; doubles from **$$$$**. **Sunset House Hotel** Oceanfront hotel with diving. 390 South Church St., George Town; 877/854-3232 or 345/949-7111; sunsethouse.com; doubles from **$$**.

WHAT TO DO

Red Sail Sports Scuba and guided dives. 345/945-5965; redsailcayman.com.

HARBOUR ISLAND

WHERE TO STAY

The Landing 7 plantation-style rooms. Bay St.; 242/333-2707; harbour islandlanding.com; doubles from **$$**.

WHERE TO SHOP

Blue Rooster Stylish accessories. King St. and Dunworth St.; 242/333-2240. **Miss Mae's** Rare items. Dunmore St.; 242/333-2002. **Sugar Mill Trading Company** Beach-wear and home design. Bay St.; 242/333-3558.

MEXICO + CENTRAL + SOUTH AMERICA

SAN MIGUEL DE ALLENDE, MEXICO

WHERE TO STAY
Casa de Sierra Nevada Luxury boutique hotel in the historic city center; 33 rooms spread over 9 colonial mansions. 35 Hospicio; 800/701-1561 or 52-415/152-7040; casadesierranevada.com; doubles from **$$**. **Dos Casas** Elegant 6-room guesthouse with a terrace overlooking church domes. 101 Quebrada; 52-415/154-4073; livingdoscasas.com; doubles from **$$**. **Hotel Posada Carmina** Old-fashioned, family-run establishment with 24 rooms. 7 Cuna de Allende; 52-415/152-8888; posada carmina.com; doubles from **$**. **The Oasis** New 4-room hotel in a 17th-century building; interiors by local firm Mitu Atelier. 1A Chiquitos; 210/745-1457; oasissanmiguel.com; doubles from **$$**.

WHERE TO EAT
Berlin Bar Convivial spot that attracts a spirited international crowd. 19 Umarán; 52-415/154-9432; dinner for two ⑪.

WHAT TO DO
Escuela de Bellas Artes Famed fine-arts school in a former 18th-century convent, with rotating exhibits. 75 Hernández Macías; 52-415/152-0289. **Galería San Miguel** The town's first

art gallery, opened in 1962, showcasing regional and national talent. 14 Plaza Principal; 52-415/152-0454. **Instituto Allende** Historic academy founded in the 1950's. 22 Ancha de San Antonio; 52-415/152-0190; instituto-allende.edu.mx. **Parroquia de San Miguel Arcángel** Late 17th-century parish church in the center of town. Jardín Principal; no phone.

LOS CABOS, MEXICO

WHERE TO STAY
Esperanza The most intimate of Cabo's high-end properties, with a private beach. Km 7 Carretera Transpeninsular, Punta Ballena; 52-624/145-6400 or 866/311-2226; esperanza resort.com; doubles from **$$$**. **Las Ventanas al Paraíso** Clutch of villas along a white-sand beach with rooftop patios and infinity pools. Km 19 Carretera Transpeninsular, San José del Cabo; 888/767-3966 or 52-624/144-2800; lasventanas.com; doubles from **$$$$**.

JALISCO, MEXICO

WHERE TO STAY
Villa Ganz A 10-room inn, minutes from Guadalajara's historic district. 1739 López Cotilla, Col. La Fayette; 800/728-9098 or 52-33/3120-1416; villaganz. com; doubles from **$$**.

WHAT TO DO
Casa 7 Leguas Houses the El Centenario distillery, where agave is crushed with a mill wheel. 360 Avda. Independencia, Atotonilco;

52-391/917-0996; tequila sieteleguas.com.mx. **Fábrica de Tequila El Llano** Old-fashioned manufacturer; tours by appointment only. 108 Calle Silverio Nuñez, Tequila; 52-374/742-0246 or 52-333/615-1646; tequila arette.com. **Los Abuelos/ Javier Sauza Museum** Ancestral Sauza hacienda. 22 Vicente Albino Rojas, Tequila; 52-347/742-1267; losabuelos.com. **Mundo Cuervo La Rojena** Sleek courtyard complex containing a distillery, tavern, and margarita bar. 75 Calle José Cuervo, Tequila; 52-374/742-2170; mundocuervo.com.

BELIZE

WHERE TO STAY
Inn at Robert's Grove Fifty-one oceanfront rooms and suites, all with private balconies. Placencia Village; 800-565-9757 or 501/523-3565; robertsgrove. com; doubles from **$$**.

OUTFITTERS
The Moorings Monohull and catamaran charters with custom itineraries. Placencia Village; 888/952-8420 or 50-1/523-3351; bareboat charters from $855 per day, with a 3- to 5-day minimum.

BOGOTÁ, COLOMBIA

WHERE TO STAY
Casa Medina Hotel National landmark from 1945 combining traditional Spanish and French architectural details. 69A-22 Carrera 7; 57-1/217-0288 or 57-1/312-0299; hotel escharleston.com; doubles from **$$**. **Charleston Bogotá Hotel** In the center of the business district, with 64 rooms. 85-46 Carrera 13; 57-1/257-1100 or 57-1/218-0590; hotelescharleston.com; doubles from **$$**. **Sofitel Bogotá Victoria Regia** Attentive staff. 85-80 Carrera 13; 57-1/621-2666; sofitel. com; doubles from **$$**.

WHAT TO DO
Teatro Colón Grand 19th-

MEXICO, CENTRAL + SOUTH AMERICA

🍽️ **DINING**   under $25 → 𝄐 $25-$74 → 𝄐𝄐 $75-$149 → 𝄐𝄐𝄐 $150-$299 → 𝄐𝄐𝄐𝄐 $300 + up → 𝄐𝄐𝄐𝄐𝄐

century theater. 5–32 Calle 10; 571/284-7420.

NIGHTLIFE

Bogotá Beer Company European-style microbrewery chain. 13-06 Calle 85; 57-1/256-6950.

PERU

WHERE TO STAY

Machu Picchu Pueblo Hotel Upscale white-washed cottages in an Andean cloud forest. Aguas Calientes; 800/442-5042 or 511/610-0410; inkaterra. com; doubles from **$$$**.

Machu Picchu Sanctuary Lodge Spanish colonial-style luxury lodge adjacent to the Incan citadel. Machu Picchu; 800/237-1236 or 511/610-8300; sanctuary lodge.net; doubles from **$$$$**. **Posada Amazonas** Eco-lodge with guided jungle excursions. 877/870-0578 or 511/421-8347; perunature.com; doubles from **$$**, all-inclusive.

Tambopata Research Center Basic guest rooms at remote field station for macaw studies. 877/870-0578; perunature.com; doubles from **$$$$**, all-inclusive.

OUTFITTERS

Inca Explorers Cuzco-based tour operator; profits go to local Andean communities. 427 Calle Ruinas; 51-84/241-070; incaexplorers. com; from $520 per person for a 5-day trip including guides, lodging, and all meals. **Lima Tours** Have been organizing trips throughout Peru since 1956. 1040 Jr. Belen; 511/619-6900; limatours.com.pe; from $523 per person for a 7-day trip, including guides, lodging, and all meals.

CHILE

WHERE TO STAY

Clos Apalta Winery Luxurious bungalows overlooking the vineyard. Higuella Villa Eloisa; 56-72/321-803; casalapostolle.com; doubles from **$$$**, all-inclusive. **Viña Matetic** Century-old estancia; on-site cheese-making operation and winery. Fundo El Rosario, Lagunillas; 56-2/232-3134; matetic.cl; doubles from **$$$**, all-inclusive.

WHAT TO DO

Viña Errázuriz Wine tasting and tours. Calle Antofagasta, Panquehue; 56-34/591-087; errazuriz.com.

EASTER ISLAND

WHERE TO STAY

Casas Rapa Nui A 9-room luxury hotel. Hotumatua St.; 866/750-6699 or 56-2/206-6060; explora.com; doubles from **$$$$$**, all-inclusive. **Hotel Hanga Roa** Ocean-front property with lively bar. Avenida Pont; 56-32/210-0299; hotelhangaroa.cl; doubles from **$$**.

PATAGONIA

WHERE TO STAY

Eolo Patagonia's Spirit An austere design, with leather sofas and 18th-century antiques. El Calafate, Argentina; 54-114/700-0075; eolo.com.ar; doubles from **$$$**, all-inclusive. **Los Cerros** A 44-room wood-and-stone luxury hostel. El Chaltén; 54-114/814-3934; loscerrosdelchalten.com; doubles from **$$$**, all-inclusive. **Remota** Industrial-inspired, U-shaped gem

facing the Seno de Última Esperanza Bay. Km 1.5, Ruta 9 N., Huerto 279, Puerto Natales, Chile; 866/431-0519 or 56-2/387-1500; remota.cl; doubles from **$$$**, all-inclusive.

SALVADOR, BRAZIL

WHERE TO STAY

Convento do Carmo Hotel Boutique property in a former convent. 800/223-6800 or 55-71/3327-8400; lhw.com; doubles from **$$$**.

WHAT TO DO

Igreja da Ordem Terceira do Carmo Church founded in 1636 and rebuilt in 1828. Largo do Carmo; no phone. **Igreja de Nossa Senhora do Rosário dos Pretos** Early-18th-century chapel, with intricate Portuguese tile covering the interior. Largo do Pelourinho; 55-71/324-5781. **Museu Afro-Brasileiro** Collection of crafts chronicling African influence on Brazilian culture. Antiga Faculdade de Medicina, Terreiro de Jesus; 55-71/3321-2013.

NIGHTLIFE

Fundo do Cravinho Samba musicians play nightly. 5 Terreiro de Jesus; 55-71/3321-7802. **O Cravinho** Famous bar, with a vast selection of cachaças. 3 Terreiro de Jesus; 55-71/3322-6759.

OUTFITTERS

Singtur City tours and visits to traditional candomblé ceremonies. 20 Praça José de Alencar, 2nd floor, Largo do Pelourinho; 55-71/3492-2212.

SÃO PAOLO, BRAZIL

WHERE TO STAY

Fasano Hotel São Paolo Modern and warm, with standout service and a rooftop spa. 88 Rua Vittorio Fasano; 55-11/3896-4000; fasano.com.br; doubles from **$$$**.

WHERE TO EAT

D.O.M. Restaurante Trailblazing Brazilian chef Alex Atala's restaurant. 549 Rua Barão de Capanema; 55-11/3088-0761; dinner for two ↑↑↑.

WHERE TO SHOP

Adriana Barra Feminine dresses in wild prints. 1801 Rua Peixoto Gomide, Casa 5; 55-11/3062-0387. **Carlos Miele** Glamorous evening wear. 2231 Rua Bela Cintra; 55-11/3065-7683. **Clube Chocolate** Minimalist 4-story shop stocked with clothing from exclusive Brazilian designers. 913 Rua Oscar Freire; 55-11/3084-1500. **Daslu** Famous luxury emporium selling everything from cars to Chanel; an entire section is dedicated to local talent. 131 Avda. Chedid Jafet; 55-11/3841-4000. **Forum Oscar Freire** All-white shop that's the brainchild of designer Tufi Duek. 916 Rua Oscar Freire; 55-11/3085-6269. **Isabela Capeto** Crafty Marc Jacobsesque women's fashions. 3358 Rua da Consolação; 55-11/3898-1878. **Pelú** Brazilian sportswear. 1257 Alameda Lorena, Casa 2; 55-11/3891-1229. **Reinaldo Lourenço** Tailored knits. 2167 Rua Bela Cintra; 55-11/3085-8150.

WESTERN EUROPE

LONDON

WHERE TO STAY

Brown's Hotel A recently renovated classic. Albemarle St.; 800/223-6800 or 44-20/7493-6020; brownshotel. com; doubles from **$$$**.
Four Seasons Hotel Canary Wharf A 10-story modern hotel on the River Thames. 46 Westferry Circus, Canary Wharf; 800/332-3442 or 44-20/7510-1999; fourseasons. com; doubles from **$$$**.

WHERE TO EAT

Bibendum Gallic-inflected seafood in the historic Michelin building. 81 Fulham Rd.; 44-20/7581-5817; dinner for two ❙❙❙❙.
Bistrotheque French-British bistro. 23–27 Wadeson St.; 44-20/8983-7900; lunch for two ❙❙❙. **Brew Wharf** House ales, brasserie dishes. Brew Wharf Yard, Stoney St.; 44-20/7378-6601; dinner for two ❙❙. **Roast** British specialties made with organic ingredients. Floral Hall, Stoney St.; 44-20/7940-1300; dinner for two ❙❙. **Scott's** Upscale seafood restaurant. 20 Mount St.; 44-20/7495-7309; lunch for two ❙❙❙. **St. John** Offbeat offerings like tripe, pigs' trotters, and offal. 26 St. John St.; 44-20/7251-0848; dinner for two ❙❙❙❙. **Tate Modern Restaurant** High-end museum restaurant, with amazing river views. Bankside; 44-20/7401-5020; dinner for two ❙❙❙. **The Wolseley** Viennese-style dining room in a former bank. 160 Piccadilly; 44-20/7499-6996; dinner for

two ❙❙❙. **Wright Brothers Oyster & Porter House** The freshest oysters in town. 11 Stoney St.; 44-20/7403-9554; dinner for two ❙❙❙.

WHERE TO SHOP

Borough Market 4½ covered acres of food stalls. 8 Southwark St.; 44-20/7407-1002. **Brindisa Spanish Foods** Fresh-pressed olive oils. 8 Stoney St., Borough Market; 44-20/8772-1036. **Dover Street Market** Avant-garde clothing, art. 17–18 Dover St.; 44-20/7518-0680. **Konditor & Cook** Whimsical cakes and pastries. 10 Stoney St.; 44-20/7407-5100. **Neal's Yard Dairy** Artisanal cheeses. 6 Park St.; 44-20/7645-3554. **Westcountry Venison** Prize-winning terrines. 3 Crown Square, Borough Market; 44-20/7407-1002.

WHAT TO DO

British Museum Vast collection of pieces from around the world. Great Russell St.; 44-20/7323-8000; thebritishmuseum. ac.uk. **Frieze Art Fair** Works from 150 cutting-edge galleries; held every October. Regent's Park; 44-20/7833-7270; friezeartfair. com. **Gagosian Contemporary** British and American art; 2 locations in London. 6–24 Britannia St.; 17–19 Davies St.; 44-20/7493-3020; gagosian.com. **Hauser & Wirth** Emerging and established artists; 2 locations in London. 196A Piccadilly St.; 92–108 Cheshire St.; 44-20/7287-2300; hauserwirth.com. **Hayward Gallery** One of the smaller institutions, with a focus on contemporary art. Belvedere Rd.; 44-2087/1663-2500;

southbankcentre.co.uk. **Monika Sprüth Philomene Magers** International art from the 60's to the present. 7A Grafton St.; 44-20/7408-1613; spruethmagers.com. **National Gallery** Impressive collection of 13th- through 20th-century paintings. Trafalgar Square; 44-20/7747-2885; national gallery.org.uk. **National Portrait Gallery** Portraits of historical and famous British figures. St. Martin's Place; 44-20/7312-2463; npg.org.uk. **Royal Academy of Arts** British art from the 18th century to the present. Burlington House, Piccadilly; 44-20/7300-8000; royal academy.org.uk. **Saatchi Gallery** Known to launch emerging artists. Duke of York's Headquarters, King's Road; 44-20/7823-2332; saatchigallery.com. **Sadie Coles** Showcases such artists as Andy Warhol and Elizabeth Peyton. 35 Heddon St.; 44-20/7434-2227; sadiecoles.com. **Serpentine Gallery** Progressive space in a public park. Kensington Gardens; 44-20/7402-6075; serpentinegallery.org.

Stuart Shave Modern Art Influential gallery. 10 Vyner St.; 44-20/8980-7742; stuart shavemodernart.com. **Tate Britain** British art from the 16th century to the present. Millbank; 44-20/7887-8888; tate.org.uk. **Tate Modern** Groundbreaking museum in an old power station. Bankside; 44-20/7887-8888; tate.org.uk. **Victoria and Albert Museum** Wide-ranging decorative-arts collections. Cromwell Rd.; 44-20/7942-2000; vam. ac.uk. **Victoria Miro Gallery** Small but important collection in a former furniture factory. 16 Wharf Rd.; 44-20/7336-8109; victoria-miro.com. **Whitechapel Gallery** Avant-garde works. 80–82 Whitechapel High St.; 44-20/7522-7888; whitechapel. org. **White Cube Gallery** Prominent gallery representing Damien Hirst and Tracey Emin; 2 locations in London. 48 Hoxton Square; 25–26 Mason's Yard; 44-20/7930-5373; whitecube.com.

NIGHTLIFE

George & Dragon A charmingly kitschy club. 2 Hackney Rd.; 44-20/

WESTERN EUROPE

DINING   under $25 → ❙ $25-$74 → ❙❙ $75-$149 → ❙❙❙ $150-$299 → ❙❙❙❙ $300 + up → ❙❙❙❙❙

7012-1100. **Golden Heart** Art-world watering hole. 110 Commercial St.; 44-20/7247-2158. **Hoxton Square Bar & Kitchen** Come for the fashionable Sunday-night party Boombox. 2–4 Hoxton Sq.; 44-20/7613-0709. **The Rake** One of London's tiniest bars, with more than 100 beers. 14A Winchester Walk; 44-20/7407-0557.

NORTHUMBER-LAND, ENGLAND

WHERE TO STAY
Macdonald Linden Hall Golf & Country Club Georgian mansion on 450 wooded acres. Longhorsley, Morpeth; 888/892-0038 or 44-1506/815-142; linden hall-hotel.co.uk; doubles from **$$**. **White Swan Hotel** 300-year-old inn, in central Alnwick. Bondgate Within, Alnwick; 44-1665/602-109; classiclodges.co.uk; doubles from **$$**, including breakfast.
WHAT TO DO
Alnwick Garden On the grounds of 12th-century Alnwick Castle, with modern water sculptures. Denwick Lane, Alnwick; 44-1665/511-350; alnwickgarden.com.

PARIS

WHERE TO STAY
Hotel Sezz Loftlike rooms, state-of-the-art baths. 6 Ave. Frémiet, 16th Arr.; 33-1/56-75-26-26; hotelsezz.com; doubles from **$$$**.
WHERE TO EAT
Boulangerie Bechu Art Deco tea room, with unusual pastries. 118 Ave. Victor Hugo, 16th Arr.; 33-1/47-27-97-79. **Gosselin**

Paris's best baguettes. 125 Rue St.-Honoré, 1st Arr.; 33-1/45-08-03-59. **La Flûte Gana** Croissants and brioches. 226 Rue des Pyrénées, 20th Arr.; 33-1/43-58-42-62. **La Maison Kayser** Flaky croissants, 60 different breads. 14 Rue Monge, 5th Arr.; 33-1/44-07-17-81. **Poilâne** Renowned wood-paneled boulangerie. 8 Rue du Cherche-Midi, 6th Arr.; 33-1/45-48-42-59.

VERSAILLES

WHERE TO STAY
Le Trianon Palace & Spa Less than a mile away from Versailles, with a pool and a spa. 1 Blvd. de la Reine; 800/228-3000 or 33-1/30-84-50-00; starwood.com; doubles from **$$$**.
WHAT TO DO
Astel Bike rentals at Grille de la Reine. La Petite Venise; 33-1/39-66-97-66. **Versailles Park** Formal gardens and fountains. Château de Versailles; 33-1/30-83-78-00; chateauversailles.fr.

LILLE, FRANCE

WHERE TO STAY
L'Hermitage Gantois 67 spacious rooms, many with beamed ceilings. 224 Rue de Paris; 33-3/20-85-30-30; hotelhermitagegantois.com; doubles from **$$**.
WHERE TO EAT
La Petite Cour Country cuisine. 17 Rue du Curé St.-Etienne; 33-3/20-51-52-81; dinner for two ❘❘. **Le Compostelle** Flemish meets French. 4 Rue St.-Etienne; 33-3/28-38-08-30; dinner for two ❘❘❘. **Méert**

Historic confectioners' shop, with delicious chocolates. 27 Rue Esquermoise; 33-3/20-57-07-44; breakfast for two ❘. **Paul** Intimate café, with creamy *chocolat chaud*, crepes, and viennoiserie. 8–12 Rue de Paris; 33-3/20-44-72-56; breakfast for two ❘.
WHERE TO SHOP
Flamant Stylish home furnishings. 59–61 Rue Esquermoise; 33-3/28-52-48-92; flamant.com.
WHAT TO DO
L'Opéra de Lille Beaux-Arts stage, opulent foyer. Place du Théâtre; 33-8/20-48-90-00; opera-lille.fr. **Palais des Beaux-Arts** Works by Rubens, Van Dyck, and Delacroix. Place de la République; 33-3/20-06-78-00.

PROVENCE

WHERE TO STAY
Chez Bru 4 rooms for rent above a 2-star restaurant. Rue de la République, Eygalières; 33-4/90-90-60-34; chezbru.com; doubles from **$$**. **Hôtel D'Europe** 16th-century mansion on the city's central square. 12 Place Crillon, Avignon; 33-4/90-14-76-76; heurope.com; doubles from **$$**. **L'Hôtel Particulier** Housed in an 18th-century pavilion. Rue de la Monnaie, Arles; 33-4/90-52-51-40; hotel-particulier.com; doubles from **$$**.
WHERE TO EAT
Bistro de France Home cooking at one of the oldest bistros in Provence. 67 Place de la Bouquerie, Apt; 33-4/90-74-22-01; lunch for two ❘❘❘. **La Charcuterie** Laid-back space, with a great charcuterie platter.

51 Rue des Arènes, Arles; 33-4/90-96-56-96; dinner for two ❘❘❘. **Le Bistrot d'Eygalières** Inventive regional cuisine popular among royalty. Rue de la République, Eygalières; 33-4/90-90-60-34; lunch for two ❘❘❘. **Le Bouquet de Basilic** Organic menu and a leafy terrace. Rte. de Murs, Gordes; 33-4/90-72-06-98; lunch for two ❘❘❘. **Le Jardin du Quai** Unadorned but sophisticated food from chef Daniel Hebet. 91 Ave. Juline-Guigue, L'Isle-sur-la-Sorgue; 33-4/90-20-14-98; lunch for two ❘❘❘. **Numéro 75** Wonderful alfresco dining. 75 Rue Guillaume Puy, Avignon; 33-4/90-27-16-00; dinner for two ❘❘❘.

BELGIUM

WHERE TO STAY
Die Swaene A set of 3 stone houses on a canal. 1 Steenhouwersdijk, Bruges; 32-50/342-798; dieswaene-hotel.com; doubles from **$$**, including breakfast. **Hotel Amigo** Flemish tapestries and Magritte prints. 1–3 Rue de l'Amigo, Brussels; 32-2/547-4747; roccoforte hotels.com; doubles from **$$$$**. **Hotel Julien** Blond-wood interiors in 2 town houses. 24 Korte Nieuw-straat, Antwerp; 32-3/229-0600; hotel-julien.com; doubles from **$$**.
WHAT TO DO
Groeninge Museum Collection of works by Bruges painters. 12 Dijver, Bruges; 32-50/448-711; brugge.be. **James Ensor House** Restored residence of the painter and print-maker. 26 Vlaanderenstraat, Ostende; 32-59/503-337.

🔑 **LODGING** under $150 → **$** $150–$299 → **$$** $300–$699 → **$$$** $700–$999 → **$$$$** $1,000 + up → **$$$$$**

Memling Museum Housed in the medieval Hospital of Saint John. 38 Mariastraat, Bruges; 32-50/448-711; brugge.be. **René Magritte Museum** Modest house with original furnishings. 135 Rue Esseghem, Brussels; 32-2/428-2626; magritte museum.be. **Royal Museum of Fine Arts** Outstanding collection covering the 14th through 20th centuries. 1–9 Leopold de Waelplaats, Antwerp; 32-3/238-7809; museum.antwerpen.be. **Rubens House** Flemish Baroque dwelling. 9–11 Wapper, Antwerp; 32-3/201-1555; museum.antwerpen. be. **St. Bavo Cathedral and Square** A Rubens master-piece, in a 16th-century cathedral. 4 Sint-Baafsplein, Ghent; 32-9/269-2045.

ANTWERP, BELGIUM

WHERE TO STAY
De Witte Lelie Hotel Row of 17th-century town houses. 16–18 Keizerstraat; 32-3/226-1966; dewittelelie. be; doubles from **$$$**. **Hilton Antwerp** In the center of the old town. Groenplaats; 800/445-8667 or 32-3/204-1212; hilton. com; doubles from **$$**.
WHERE TO SHOP
Adelin Vintage diamonds. 6–8 Steenhouwersvest; 32-3/234-9552. **Diamond House** Unassuming shop with a skillful dealer. 59 Vesting-straat; 32-3/226-9393. **Diamondland** Salesrooms and guided tours at the city's largest diamond store. 33A Appelmansstraat; 32-3/229-2990. **Katz Jewellers** Well-respected, experienced dealer. 19 Appelmansstraat;

32-3/231-9780.

AMSTERDAM

WHERE TO STAY
Grand Amsterdam Refurbished 17th-century convent with a hammam. 197 Oudezijds Voorburgwal; 800/763-4835 or 31-20/555-3111; sofitel.com; doubles from **$$$**.
WHERE TO SHOP
Droog Design Renowned collective's showroom. 7b Staalstraat; 31-20/523-5059. **Frozen Fountain** Furniture, kitchenware, and a large selection of Royal Tichelaar porcelain. 645 Prinsen-gracht; 31-20/622-9375. **Pol's Potten** Cavernous housewares emporium, with handcrafted furniture. 39 KNSM-laan; 31-20/419-3541. **WonderWood** Gallery-cum-shop. 3 Rusland; 31-20/625-3738.

STOCKHOLM

WHERE TO STAY
Rival Hotel Boutique property launched by ABBA star Benny Andersson. 3 Mariatorget; 46-8/5457-8900; rival.se; doubles from **$$$**.
WHERE TO EAT
Bakficka Upscale Swedish by local celebrity chef. 4 Fredrikshovsgatan; 46-8/660-1599; dinner for two ¶¶¶. **Gondolen** French cuisine, and uninterrupted city views. 6 Stadsgården; 46-8/641-7090; dinner for two ¶¶¶. **KB** Traditional dishes like herring and elk, served in a 1931 dining room. 7 Smålandsgatan; 46-8/679-6032; dinner for two ¶¶¶. **Lux** Minimalist space with Nordic concoctions.

116 Primusgatan; 46-8/619-0190; dinner for two ¶¶¶¶. **Riche** Sleek, modern interior. 4 BirgerJarlsgatan; 46-8/5450-3560; dinner for two ¶¶¶. **Riddarbageriet** Small bakery with room for only 6 or 8 people. 15 Riddargatan; 46-8/660-3375; lunch for two ¶. **Vinbaren** Local hot spot by Erik Lallerstedt. 6 Stadsgården; 46-8/5569-6066; dinner for two ¶¶¶.

COLOGNE, GERMANY

WHERE TO STAY
Hopper St. Antonius 54 rooms decorated with original photography. 32 Dagobertstrasse; 49-221/16600; hopper.de; doubles from **$$**. **Hotel Santo** A modern oasis of calm in the middle of the city. 22–26 Dagobertstrasse; 49-221/913-9770; hotel santo.de; doubles from **$$**. **Hotel im Wasserturm** Centrally located former water tower. 2 Kaygasse; 49-221/20080; hotel-im-wasserturm.de; doubles from **$$$**.
WHERE TO EAT
Vintage Teutonic wines and digestifs to accompany seasonal dishes. 31–35 Pfeilstrasse; 49-221/920-710; dinner for two ¶¶¶¶.
WHERE TO SHOP
Apropos Coeln Designer for him and her. 12 Mittelstras-se; 49-221/272-5190. **Atelier Ludvik** Funky selections from designer Fenja Ludwig. 43 Palmstrasse; 49-221/277-4568. **Perla Zayek** Evening dresses by a Lebanese-born designer. 94 Friesenwall; 49-221/256-022. **Walter Koenig** Extensive collection

of photo books. 4 Ehren-strasse; 49-221/205-960.

LEIPZIG, GERMANY

WHERE TO STAY
Hotel Fürstenhof Restored 18th-century mansion, a 5-minute walk from the Museum der Bildenden Künste. 8 Tröndlinring; 800/325-3589 or 49-341/140-370; luxurycollection. com; doubles from **$$**. **Seaside Park Hotel** Art Deco hotel. 7 Richard-Wagner-Strasse; 49-341/98520; park-hotel-leipzig.de; doubles from **$$**.
WHERE TO EAT
Café Neubau Soups and sandwiches in a contempo-rary art space. 11 Karl-Tauchnitz-Strasse; 49-341/140-8120; lunch for two ¶.
WHAT TO DO
Galerie Eigen + Art Influential gallery in the Spinnerei complex. 5 Halle; 49-341/960-7886; eigen-art.com. **Galerie für Zeitgenössische Kunst (GfZK)** Artists from former Soviet Bloc countries and Leipzig. 9–11 Karl-Tauchnitz-Strasse; 49-341/140-810; gfzk.de. **Leipzig Academy of Visual Arts** School with an on-site gallery that displays student work. 11 Wächerstrasse; 49-341/213-5133; hgb-leipzig. de. **Museum der Bildenden Künste** Everything from 17th-century Dutch paintings to Leipzig School canvases. 10 Katharinen-strasse; 49-341/216-990; mdbk.de. **Pierogi Leipzig** Sattelite of the Williams-burg, Brooklyn–based Pierogi gallery. 10 Halle;

DINING   under $25 → ¶ $25-$74 → ¶¶ $75-$149 → ¶¶¶ $150-$299 → ¶¶¶¶ $300 + up → ¶¶¶¶¶

49-341/241-9080; pierogi 2000.com. **Spinnerei** Early 19th-century cotton mills renovated into art spaces and studios. 7 Spinnerei strasse; spinnerei.de.

AUSTRIA

WHERE TO STAY
Hotel Elefant 400-year-old inn with a legendary wine cellar. 4 Sigmund-Haffner-Gasse, Salzburg; 43-662/843-397; elefant.at; doubles from **$$**. **Palais Coburg** All-suite hotel. 4 Coburgbastei, Vienna; 800/735-2478 or 43-1/518-180; palais-coburg.com; doubles from **$$$$**.

WHAT TO DO
Mozarthaus Vienna An exhibition center devoted to the composer, in a 17th-century house where he once lived. 5 Domgasse, Vienna; 43-1/512-1791; mozarthausvienna.at. **Mozarts Geburtshaus** Composer's birthplace, now a museum on a busy shopping street. 9 Getreide-gasse, Salzburg; 43-662/844-313; mozarteum.at. **Salzburger Festspiele** Salzburg's famed annual summer festival of operas, concerts, and plays. 43-662/804-5206; salzburgfestival.at. **Theater an der Wien** New stagings of Mozart operas. 6 Linke Wienzeile, Vienna; 43-1/ 5883-0660; theater-wien.at.

PIEDMONT, ITALY

WHERE TO STAY
Hotel Castello di Sinio Luxurious property run by a knowledgeable American couple with a passion for food and wine. 1 Vicolo Castello, Sinio; 39-0173/263-889; hotelcastellodisinio.com; doubles from **$$**. **Marchesi Alfieri** Farmhouse on the grounds of a winery. 28 Piazza Alfieri, San Martino Alfieri, Asti; 39-0141/976-015; marchesi alfieri.it; doubles from **$**.

WHERE TO EAT
Grom New-school gelateria that sources all its own ingredients. 1/D Piazza Paleocapa, Turin; 39-011/511-9067. **I Bologna** Owned by an esteemed Bologna wine-making family. 4 Via Nicola Sardi, Rocchetta Tanaro; 39-0141/644-600; dinner for two ❙❙. **La Bottega del Vicoletto** Dishes to go, including area cheeses and rare provisions such as venison prosciutto. 6 Via Bertero, Alba; 39-0173/363-196. **Osteria de la Rosa Rossa** Seriously delicious snails; book early. 31 Via San Pietro, Cherasco; 39-0172/488-133; dinner for two ❙❙❙. **Osteria LaLibera** Inventive preparations of market-fresh ingredients. 24A Via Elvio Pertinace, Alba; 39-0173/293-155; dinner for two ❙❙❙.

WHERE TO SHOP
Enoteca Regionale del Barolo Sommeliers pour wines from a cross section of Barolo's producers. Castello Falletti, Barolo; 39-0173/56277; baroloworld.it.

LE MARCHE, ITALY

WHERE TO STAY
Hotel Emilia Glamorous hotel overlooking the Adriatic Sea. Poggio di Portonovo, Ancona; 39-071/801-145; hotelemilia.com; doubles from **$$$**. **Le Marche Explorer Rental Properties** Company with extraordinary selection of restored farmhouses, convents, and apartments to rent by the week. 39-733/694-352; le-marche-explorer.com; one-bedroom apartments from **$**. **Palazzo dalla Casapiccola** 10 suites in a 1600's mansion. 2 Piazzola Vincenzo Gioberti; 39-071/757-4818. palazzodallacasapiccola.it; doubles from **$$**.

WHERE TO EAT
Uliassi Seaside fish restaurant specializing in fried octopus and squid-ink pasta. 6 Banchina di Levante, Senigallia; 39-071/65463; uliassi.it; dinner for two ❙❙❙❙.

WHAT TO DO
Abbadia di Chiaravalle di Fiastra A 12th-century abbey. Via Abbadia di Fiastra, Tolentino. **Cathedral of San Ciriaco** Hilltop chapel overlooking the Adriatic, with a painting of the Virgin said to protect travelers from storms at sea. Monte Guasco, Ancona. **Church of Santa Maria a Pié di Chienti** Romanesque church from the 10th century. Montecosaro, Macerata; 39-073/386-5241. **Church of Santa Maria in Telusiano** Altarpiece features Lorenzo Lotto's *Crucifixion*. Monte San Giusto, Macerata. **Galleria Nazionale delle Marche** Paintings by Paolo Uccello and Piero della Francesca. Palazzo Ducale, 3 Piazza Duca Federico, Urbino; 39-072/22760. **Museo Villa Colloredo Mels** Lorenzo Lotto's *Annunciation* is on display here. Recanati; 39-071/757-0410. **Santa Casa and Basilica** The Holy House of the Black Madonna. Palazzo Apostolico, Piazza della Madonna, Loreto; 39-071/970-104.

ROME

WHERE TO STAY
Casa Howard Affordable design hotel a short taxi ride from Testaccio and Esquilino. 18 Vin Capo le Case, Piazza del Popolo; 39-06/6992-4555; casa howard.com; doubles from **$$**. **Radisson SAS Es. Hotel** Futuristic-looking property. 171 Via Filippo Turati; 800/333-3333 or 39-06/444-841; radissonsas.com; doubles from **$$$**.

WHERE TO EAT
Sora Rosa Simple local dishes. 74 Via di Tor Carbone; 39-06/718-8453; dinner for two ❙❙. **Trattoria Monti** The food of the Le Marche region. 13 Via di San Vito; 39-06/446-6573; dinner for two ❙❙❙. **Volpetti Deli** Cramped space filled with cheeses and meats. 47 Via Marmorata; 39-06/574-2352; snacks for two ❙.

WHAT TO DO
Chiesa di Santa Bibiana Small, beautiful church with a 17th-century Bernini façade. 154 Via Giovanni Giolitti; no phone. **Metaverso** Club with reggae, electronica, and drum 'n' bass. 38A Via di Monte Testaccio; 39-06/574-4712. **Museo d'Arte Contemporanea di Roma (MACRO Future), Mattatoio** A branch of Rome's modern-art museum, in a former slaughterhouse on Monte

LODGING under $150 → **$** $150-$299 → **$$** $300-$699 → **$$$** $700-$999 → **$$$$** $1,000 + up → **$$$$$**

Testaccio. 4 Piazza Orazio Giustiniani; 39-06/6710-70400; macro.roma.museum. **Pyramid of Caius Cestius** A Roman magistrate's 12 B.C. tomb. Near Piazza di Porta San Paolo; no phone. **Testaccio Market** One of Rome's liveliest. Piazza Testaccio; no phone.

NAPLES, ITALY

WHERE TO STAY
Chiaja Hotel de Charme Friendly staff and a convenient location. 216 Via Chiaia; 39-081/415-555; hotelchiaia.it; doubles from **$$**. **Hotel Excelsior** A luxe property overlooking the water. 48 Via Partenope; 800/325-3589 or 39-081/764-0111; starwood.com; doubles from **$$$**.
WHERE TO EAT
Europeo Mattozzi Among the city's best—and best-loved—restaurants. 4 Via Campodisola Marchese; 39-081/552-1323; dinner for two ❙❙❙. **Gusto & Gusto** Italian dishes, served in a waterfront setting. Via Partenope; 39-081/245-2662; dinner for two ❙❙.
WHERE TO SHOP
Borrelli Famous for men's wear. 68 Via Filangieri; 39-081/423-8273. **Eddy Monetti** Men's and women's clothes. 45 Via dei Mille; 39-081/407-064. **E. Marinella** The source for ties. 287A Riviera di Chiaia; 39-081/764-4214. **Gay-Odin** The city's top *cioccolateria*; multiple locations. 37 Via Cervantes; 39-081/562-8068. **Magnifique** Custom-made and ready-to-wear men's clothes. 37C Via

Filangieri; 39-081/421-940. **Milord** Hip men's wear. 53 Vico Cavallerizza; 39-081/422-982. **Nino di Nicola** Men's suits. 69 Via Santa Caterina; 39-081/404-349.
WHAT TO DO
Basilio Liverino Fascinating coral museum. 61 Via Montedoro, Torre del Greco; 39-081/881-1225. **Capodimonte Museum** Neoclassical palace, with Dutch, Spanish, and Italian art. 1 Via Miano, Porta Piccola; 39-081/749-9110. **Cathedral of Naples** Baroque frescoes and 4th-century mosaics in the baptistery. 147 Via del Duomo; 39-081/449-097. **Certosa-Museo di San Martino** Monastery turned museum. 5 Largo San Martino; 39-081/578-1769. **Museo d'Arte Contemporanea Donna Regina** Museum devoted to international contemporary art, in a 17th-century palace. 79 Via Settembrini; 39-081/292-833; museomadre.it. **National Archaeological Museum** The world's best collections of Greek and Roman antiquities. 19 Piazza Museo; 39-081/440-166; archeona.arti.beniculturali.it.

BARCELONA

WHERE TO STAY
Hotel Omm Undulating façade and pitch-black corridors. 265 Rosselló; 34/93-445-4000; hotelomm.es; doubles from **$$$**.
WHERE TO SHOP
Adolfo Dominguez Office-ready trousers and dinner-worthy skirts. 89 Passeig de Gràcia; 34/93-215-1339. **Agatha Ruiz de la Prada** Bright-hued women's

clothes. 314–16 Consell de Cent; 34/93-487-1667. **Agua del Carmen** Offbeat dresses. 5 Carr. Bonaire; 34/93-268-7799. **Atram** Toile cushions and more. 19 Rambla del Prat; 34/93-237-5297. **Beatriz Furest** Hip clothes and handbags. 1 Esparteria; 34/93-268-3796. **Carolina Herrera** City sneakers and pretty dresses. 87 Passeig de Gràcia; 34/93-272-1584. **Cereria Subirà** Unique candles. 7 Baixada Llibreteria; 34/93-315-2606. **Corium** Well-edited accessories. 106 Passeig de Gràcia; 34/93-217-5575. **Custo Barcelona** Stretchy, cheerful tops. 7 Plaça de les Olles; 34/93-268-7893. **La Cova del Col. leccionisme** Magazines dating from the 1920's and vintage postcards. 15 Carr. Sta. Eugénia; 34/93-500-8505. **La Manual Alpargatera** Espadrilles. 7 Carr. Avinyó; 34/93-301-0172. **Sare: Artesanías de África** Inexpensive bangles. 16 Carr. Sta. Eugénia; 34/93-217-8942. **Vinçon** Groovy home-design store. 96 Passeig de Gràcia; 34/93-215-6050.

ELCIEGO, SPAIN

WHERE TO STAY
Hotel Marqués de Riscal Frank Gehry–designed architectural masterpiece on a vineyard. 1 Calle Torrea; 800/325-3589 or 34/945-180-880; luxurycollection.com; doubles from **$$$$$**.
WHERE TO EAT
La Cueva Local favorite. 36 Calle Barrihuelo; 34/945-606-440; dinner for two ❙❙.

WHAT TO DO
Iglesia de San Andrés A 16th-century church in the center of town. 34/945-606-038. **Vinoteca La Ermita** Gourmet food and wine. 7 Plaza Mayor; 34/686-863-207.

GIJÓN, SPAIN

WHERE TO STAY
Hotel Don Manuel Basic hotel, conveniently located. 4 Linares Rivas; 34/985-171-313; doubles from **$$**.
WHAT TO DO
Semana Negra Festival Weeklong annual summer literary festival. 34/985-339-800; semananegra.org.

AEGEAN CRUISE

EasyCruise Budget ship that departs from Athens for regular excursions in the Greek islands. 30-211/211-6211; easycruise.com; from **$** per night.

CHIOS, GREECE

WHERE TO STAY
Argentikon High-end hotel with 8 suites, most in private buildings. Argenti Giazou St., Kambos; 30-227/103-3111; argentikon.gr; doubles from **$$$$$**, including breakfast. **Chios Chandris** Quiet balconies and views of the port. 2nd Eugenia's Chandris St., Chios Town; 30-227/104-4401; handris.gr; doubles from **$$**.
WHERE TO EAT
O Kambos Popular taverna. Kambos; 30-227/103-2855; dinner for two ❙.

EASTERN EUROPE

BULGARIA

WHERE TO STAY
House Djambazki
Family-run guesthouse.
53 Iskar Blvd., Govedartsi;
359-88/857-3133; house-
djambazki.com; doubles
from **$**. **Rila Monastery**
Monks' cells, some with
shared bathrooms. Rilska
River Vally, Rila; 359/
7054-2208; individual beds
from **$**.

WHAT TO DO
Musala At 9,600 feet,
the tallest mountain
in the Balkans. There are
several routes to the top,
including a gondola from
a nearby ski town; Borovets
Ski Resort; 359/722-661.
Rila National Park
More than 100,000 forested
acres, with granite peaks,
waterfalls, and mountain
streams. 359/707-3302;
rilanationalpark.org.
Seven Lakes Alpine
glacial lakes, accessible
from the towns of Zeleni
Preslap and Mal'ovitsa.
Rila National Park Visitors
Center, Sapareva Banya;
359/707-3302.

MONTENEGRO

WHERE TO STAY
Hotel Splendid 188 rooms
overlooking the Adriatic Sea,
in Becici village. Becici;
381-86/773-777; montenegro
stars.com; doubles from **$$$**.
Sveti Stefan Famous luxury
island resort with a compact
complex of red-roofed stone
buildings, reopening as an
Aman resort in 2008. 3 miles
south of Budva, across a

causeway; 800/477-9180
or 656/887-3337;
amanresorts.com.

TOUR OPERATOR
Butterfield & Robinson
Private yachting itineraries.
800/678-1147 or 416/864-
1354; butterfield.com;
from $16,900 for a 10-day
trip for two.

HUNGARY

WHERE TO STAY
Betekints Hotel On the
east end of Lake Balaton,
with spacious rooms.
4 Veszprémvölgyi St.,
Veszprém; 36-88/579-280;
betekints.hu; doubles from
$. **Four Seasons Hotel
Gresham Palace** A
soaring Art Nouveau
masterpiece, less than 2
hours from the Lake

Balaton wine region.
5–6 Roosevelt Square,
Budapest; 800/332-
3442 or 36-1/268-6000;
fourseasons.com; doubles
from **$$$**.

WHERE TO EAT
Hotel Bacchus
Authentic local dishes
in a subterranean room
attached to an 18th-
century wine cellar.
18 Erzsébet Királyné St.,
Keszhely; 36-83/510-450;
dinner for two ¶¶. **Szent
Orbán Borház** Traditional
Hungarian food in a
vineyard setting. 5 Kisfaludy
St., Badacsony; 36-30/233-
0398; dinner for two ¶¶.

WHAT TO DO
Figula Wines Modern
winery on an ancient site.
44B Siske St., Balatonfüred;
36-87/481-661; figula.hu.
Szeremley Estate One of

the most scenic places to
try Hungaricum wine. 51–53
Fö St., Badacsonytomaj;
36-87/571-210.

UKRAINE

WHERE TO STAY
Evpatoria Hotel 2 large,
modern buildings near
a private beach. 1/64
Pobeda St., Evpatoria; 38-
065/695-1418; doubles
from **$**. **Planeta** Faces
the Black Sea and Moinaki
Lake, with 142 rooms.
29/73 Kositsky St.,
Evpatoria; 38-065/692-
8070; doubles from **$**.

WHAT TO DO
Kazantip Festival
Monthlong dissident
dance party on the
Crimean peninsula.
Kazantip; kazantip.com

LODGING | under $150 → **$** $150-$299 → **$$** $300-$699 → **$$$** $700-$999 → **$$$$** $1,000 + up → **$$$$$**

RIGA, LATVIA

WHERE TO STAY
Hotel Bergs Upscale property in 19th-century building with terraces. 83/85 Elizabetes St.; 371/777-0900; hotelbergs. lv; doubles from **$$**.

WHERE TO EAT
Vincent's The city's power-lunch spot. 19 Elizabetes St.; 371/733-2634; dinner for two ¶¶¶.

WHERE TO SHOP
Bergs Bazaar The best shopping district. 13/4 Marijas St.; 371/750-2310. **Garage** Housewares and accessories. 83/85 Elizabetes St.; 371/672-88308.

NIGHTLIFE
Club Essential Multiple dance floors. 2 Skolas St.; 371/724-2289.

SOCHI, RUSSIA

WHERE TO STAY
Grand Hotel Rodina Acres of creamy marble, and manicured grounds leading down to a private beachfront. 33 Vinogradnaya St.; 7-8622/539-000; grandhotelrodina.com; doubles from **$$$**.

WHAT TO DO
Ordzhonikidze Sanatorium Stalin-era health spa in a historic building. 96/5 Kurortny Propekt; 7-8622/976-657. **Kinotavr Film Festival** 10-day event held each June. 2 Teatralnaya St.; 7-495/916-9060; kinotavr. ru. **Zelyonaya Roscha Hotel at Stalin's Dacha** Kitschy museum; requires advance reservations, which a hotel can arrange.

120 Kurortniy Ave.; 7-8622/695-330.

TOUR OPERATOR
Exeter International Provides travel advice and local arrangements. 800/633-1008 or 813/251-5355; exeterinternational. com; from $3,000 a day for a 3-day trip for two.

NOVGOROD, RUSSIA

WHERE TO STAY
Volkhov Hotel Recently renovated landmark. 24 Predtechenskaya St.; 7-8162/335-505; doubles from **$**.

WHAT TO DO
Cathedral of Our Lady of the Sign 17th-century monument near the Volkhov River. Ilyin St.; no phone. **Cathedral of Saint Sophia** Byzantine church. 11 Kremlin; 7-8162/773-556. **Fine Arts Museum** Collection of medieval icons. 2 Sophiskaya Square; 7-8162/772-265. **Kremlin Walled City** 30-acre brick-walled city surrounded by guard towers. 5 Sennaya Square; 7-8162/773-074; eng.tourism.velikiy novgorod.ru. **Vitoslavlitsy Museum of Wooden Architecture and Yurievsky Monastery** Beautiful centuries-old log structures, some with seamless dovetailed corners. Yurevskoe Shosse; 7-8162/778-160. **Yaroslavsky Court** Ruins of the former rulers' palace complex. East bank of the Volkhov River near the market; no phone.

Alexandria
Tel Aviv
Cairo
Rabat
Morocco
—Israel
Egypt
U.A.E.
Duba
Oman

AFRICA
+
THE MIDDLE EAST

Tanzania

Mozambique
•Maputo
South Africa

AFRICA + THE MIDDLE EAST

CAIRO, EGYPT

WHERE TO STAY
Four Seasons Cairo at Nile Plaza Elegant 30-story hotel on the bank of the Nile. 1089 Corniche El Nil, Garden City; 800/332-3442 or 20-2/2791-7000; fourseasons.com; doubles from **$$$**. **Talisman Hotel de Charme** Downtown boutique property. 39 Talaat Harb St.; 20-2/2393-9431; doubles from **$**.

WHERE TO EAT
Felfela Savory Egyptian staples. 15 Hoda Sharaawi St.; 20-2/2392-2833; dinner from ¶¶.

WHAT TO DO
Mashrabia Gallery Established, independent gallery. 8 Champollion St.;

20-2/2578-4494; mashrabia gallery.com. **Townhouse Gallery of Contemporary Art** Cutting-edge exhibitions. 10 Nabrawy St.; 20-2/2576-8086; thetownhouse gallery.com.

ALEXANDRIA, EGYPT

WHERE TO STAY
Four Seasons San Stefano 118 rooms on the site of a 1930's resort. 399 El Giesh Rd., San Stefano Grand Plaza; 800/332-3442 or 20-3/469-0141; four seasons.com; doubles from **$$$**.

WHAT TO DO
Alexandria National Museum Art and artifacts from two millennia. 110 El-Horreyya Road; 20-3/483-5519. **Bibliotheca Alexandrina** Re-creation of the fabled library. El Chatby; 20-3/483-9999; bibalex.org.

RABAT, MOROCCO

WHERE TO STAY
Dar Al Batoul The rooms encircle a courtyard. 7 Derb Jirari; 212-37/727-250; riadbatoul.com; doubles from $.

WHAT TO DO
Chellah Gardens Roman and Muslim ruins in a tranquil setting, in the outskirts of Rabat's Ville Nouvelle (the modern section). 212-37/673-918. **Old Town** Walled medina with shopping bazaars. South of Republic Street; no phone.

TANZANIA

OUTFITTERS
George Mavroudis Safaris Custom, private, luxury tented safaris. 255-27/254-8840; gmsafaris.com; from $10,000 per person for a 7-day trip. **Hoopoe Safaris** High-end cultural experiences. 800/408-3100 or 255-27/250-7011; hoopoe.com; from $2,425 per person for an 8-day trip. **IntoAfrica** Value-priced excursions. 44-114/255-5610; intoafrica.co.uk; from $1,645 per person for a 7-day trip.

MAPUTO, MOZAMBIQUE

WHERE TO STAY
Serena Polana Hotel Portuguese-colonial grandeur by the Indian Ocean. 1380 Avda. Julius Nyerere; 258-21/491-001; serenahotels.com; doubles from $$.

WHERE TO EAT
Café Camissa Outdoor spot that draws artists and journalists. 194 Rua de Argélia;

258-82/415-3100; snacks for two ❢. **Catembe Gallery Hotel** Maputo's best Sunday brunch. Catembe Jetty; 258-21/380-0501; brunch for two ❢. **Clube Naval** Curry dishes and wines served poolside. 1866 Avda. Marginal; dinner for two ❢❢❢. **Costa do Sol** Ocean-front grill house. 10429 Avda. Marginal; 258-21/450-115; lunch for two ❢❢. **Fish Market** Vendors grill the catch of the day. Avda. Marginal and Rua Palma; no phone; lunch for two ❢.

SOUTH AFRICA

WHERE TO STAY
CC Africa Phinda Private Game Reserve 4-day bush-skills courses. KwaZulu-Natal; 888/882-3742 or 27-21/532-5800; ccafrica.com; course from $335; doubles from $$$ per person.

OUTFITTERS
Abercrombie & Kent Customized ranger training. 800/554-7094; abercrombiekent.com; from $700 per day per person. **Bushcamp Company and Mfuwe Lodge** Basic courses. Mfuwe, Zambia; 260/624-6041 or 871-76/228-0123; bushcampcompany.com; from $3,750 per person for a 7-day course. **EcoTraining** Learn about tracking and animal habitats. Makuleke and Karongwe Camps; 27-13/745-7777; from $2,494 per person for a 28-day course.

TEL AVIV, ISRAEL

WHERE TO STAY
Nina Café Suites Hotel 4 Art Deco–style rooms. 29 Shabazi St., Neve Tzedek;

972-52/508-4141; ninacafehotel.com; doubles from $$.

WHERE TO SHOP
Delicatessen Unconventional fashions and handmade jewelry. 4 Barzilai St.; 972-3/560-2297. **Frau Blau** Clothes with a vintage edge. 8 Ha'Hashmal St.; 972-3/560-1735. **Nait** Asian-inspired women's dresses. 10 Mikve Israel St.; 972-3/560-0402. **Shani Bar** Shoes and Italian leather accessories. 3 Mikve Israel St.; 972-3/560-5981.

DUBAI, U.A.E.

WHERE TO STAY
Al Qasr Resort with more than 40 bars and restaurants, and a large souk. Jumeirah Beach; 877/854-8051 or 971-4/366-8888; madinatjumeirah.com; doubles from $$$$. **Bab Al Shams Desert Resort and Spa** Luxe oasis with falconry shows and desert cruising. Endurance City; 971-4/832-6699; jumeirahbabalshams.com; doubles from $$$. **Burj Al Arab** Over-the-top luxury. Jumeirah Beach; 877/854-8051 or 971-4/301-7777; burj-al-arab.com; doubles from $$$$$. **One & Only Royal Mirage** 65-acre coastal property including the Residence and Spa, a 49-suite enclave on a private beach. Jumeirah Beach; 866/552-0001 or 971-4/399-9999; oneandonlyresorts.com; doubles from $$$$. **Park Hyatt** Just opened on Dubai Creek, with a modern-Arabian theme. 800/778-7477 or 971-4/602-1234; dubai.park.hyatt.com; doubles from $$$.

WHERE TO EAT
SHO CHO Sushi restaurant and nightclub. Dubai Marine Beach Resort & Spa, Jumeirah Beach; 971-4/346-1111; dinner for two ❢❢.

WHERE TO SHOP
Artspace New exhibitions of contemporary art each month. Fairmont Hotel Dubai, Sheikh Zayed Rd.; 971-4/332-5523. **Five Green** Concept store-gallery holds avant-garde shows and performances. Garden Home Bldg., Oud Metha Rd.; 971-4/336-4100. **Harvey Nichols** Marble-bedecked complex, with great selection of designer labels. Mall of the Emirates, Sheikh Zayed Rd.; 971-4/409-8888. **Mall of the Emirates** Retail behemoth. Sheikh Zayed Rd.; 971-4/409-9000. **S*uce** Boutique with clothes by Middle Eastern designers. Village Mall, Jumeirah Beach; 971-4/344-7270. **Third Line** Gallery with film screenings. 3 Al Quoz; 971-4/341-1367. **Villa Moda** Luxury shopping destination within a mall. Sheikh Zayed Rd.; 971-4/330-4555. **XVA** Modern art, plus a café. Bastakiya, 971-4/353-5383.

WHAT TO DO
Nad Al Sheba Racetrack World-class facility. Off Al Ain Rd.; 971-4/332-2277; dubairacingclub.com.

OMAN

WHERE TO STAY
Shangri-La's Barr Al Jissah Resort & Spa On a pristine stretch of white sand. Qantab Road, Muscat; 866/565-5050 or 968/2477-6666; doubles from $$$.

ASIA

Manchuria
Hokkaido
Mongolia
Japan
Shikoku
China
Macau • Guangzhou
India
ASIA
Sri Lanka
Vietnam
Kuala Lumpur
Singapore
Bali

ASIA

MONGOLIA

WHERE TO STAY
Three Camel Lodge High-end desert camp of 46 yurts. Bulgan Village, South Gobi; 800/998-6634 or 609/860-9008; threecamel lodge.com; doubles from **$**.

WHAT TO DO
Choijin Lama Temple One of the country's best collections of Buddhist art. 7 Genden St., Ulaanbaatar; no phone. **Erdene Zuu Khiid** Mongolia's oldest monastery. Ovorkhangai Aimag, Kharakhorum Sum; no phone. **Gandan Monastery** Active religious center with 500 practicing monks. Zanabazar St., Ulaanbaatar; 976-11/360-233; gandan.mn.

TOUR OPERATORS
Geographic Expeditions Adventure-oriented tours from the Gobi Desert to Lake Khövsghöl. 800/777-8183 or 415/922-0448; geoex.com; from $4490 per person for an 18-day trip. **Mountain Travel Sobek** Moderately difficult trekking. 888/687-6235 or 510/594-6000; mtsobek. com; from $5,095 per person for a 15-day trip. **Nomadic Expeditions** More than two dozen options. 800/998-6634 or 609/860-9008; nomadicexpeditions. com; from $6,000 for two people for a 13-day trip.

MANCHURIA, CHINA

WHERE TO STAY
Kempinski Hotel Dalian Glass high-rise with 457 rooms overlooking the city and a park. 92 Jiefang Rd., Dalian; 800/426-3135 or 86-411/8259-8888; kempinski. com; doubles from **$**. **Hotel Moderne** 1906 landmark near the Songhua River. 89 Zhong-yang St., Harbin; 86-451/488-4000; doubles from **$**.

WHAT TO DO
Church of St. Sophia Largest Russian Orthodox church in Asia. Toulong Jie St., Harbin; 86-451/8468-6904. **9.18 Museum** Exhibits on the Mukden Incident. 46 Wanghua Nan St., Shenyang; 86-24/2271-0337. **Victory Plaza** One of China's biggest malls. Tianjin St., Dalian; no phone.

MACAU, CHINA

WHERE TO STAY
Hotel Lisboa Modern hotel with a traditional Chinese casino. 2–4 Avda. de Lisboa; 853-2/888-3888; hotelisboa. com; doubles from **$$**. **Wynn Macau** Bronzed-glass tower. Rua Cidade de Sintra, NAPE; 853-2/888-9966; wynnmacau.com; doubles from **$$$**.

WHAT TO DO
Fisherman's Wharf Sprawling waterfront mall. Avda. da Amizade; 853-2/993-300. **Sands Casino** Over-the-top, 3-level casino with 4 restaurants. 203 Largo de Monte Carlo; 853-2/888-3388; sands.com.mo.

GUANGZHOU, CHINA

WHERE TO STAY
Garden Hotel 828-room skyscraper with great restaurants. 368 Huanshi Dong St.; 86-20/8333-8989; thegardenhotel.com. cn; doubles from **$$**.

WHERE TO EAT
Peach Blossom Restaurant The city's best dim sum. 368 Huanshi Dong Rd.; 86-20/8333-8989; lunch for two **❙❙**. **Yumin Restaurant** Fresh seafood plucked straight from dining room tanks. 559-567 Yingbin Rd., Dashi Town, Panyu; 86-20/2287-8811; dinner for two **❙**.

WHAT TO DO
Qingping Market Maze of more than 2,000 stalls. Qingping St. and Tiyun St., Shamian Island; no phone.

SHIKOKU, JAPAN

WHERE TO STAY
Utoco Deep Sea Therapy Center & Hotel Minimalist décor; deep-sea treatments. 6969-1 Murotomisaki-cho,

Muroto City, Kochi; 81-8/8722-1811; utocods.co.jp; doubles from **$$**.

HOKKAIDO, JAPAN

WHERE TO STAY
Windsor Hotel Toya Resort & Spa Full-service resort. Shimizu, Abuta-cho, Abuta-gun; 800/745-8883 or 81-142/731-111; windsor-hotels.co.jp; doubles from **$$$**.
WHAT TO DO
Shikotsu-Toya National Park Lakes and active volcanoes. Sapporo; 810-14/275-2446; mptourism.com.

INDIA

WHERE TO STAY
Hotel Chandela 90 ornate rooms within expansive gardens. Airport Rd., Khajuraho; 866/969-1825 or 91-768/627-2355; taj hotels.com; doubles from **$**. **Oberoi Amarvilas** Moorish-influenced luxury hotel. Taj East Gate, Agra; 800/562-3764 or 91-562/223-1515; oberoihotels.com; doubles from **$$$$**. **Raj Niwas Palace** 7 grand suites with peacocks wandering the grounds. Dholpur; 91-11/2643-6572; dholpur palace.com; doubles from **$$**. **Sheesh Mahal** Converted medieval palace hotel within a historic complex. Orchha; 91-768/025-2624; mptourism.com; doubles from **$**. **Usha Kiran Palace** Intimate, newly renovated 120-year-old building. Jayendraganj, Lashkar, Gwalior; 866/969-1825 or 91-751/244-4000; tajhotels.com; doubles from **$$**.
WHAT TO DO
Gwalior Fort Fortified city.

Lashkar, Gwalior; no phone. **Jai Vilas Palace** Royal residence and museum. Lashkar, Gwalior; no phone. **Lakshmana Temple** Carved sandstone shrine. Khajuraho; no phone. **Orchha** Hindu and Islamic palaces. Orchha; no phone.
TOUR OPERATORS
Cox & Kings Upscale tours. 800/999-1758; coxandkingsusa.com; from $2,834 per person for a 13-day trip. **India Safaris and Tours** Delhi-based company partly owned by CC Africa. 91-11/2680-7750; indiasafaris.com; from $8365 per person for a 12-day trip.

SRI LANKA

WHERE TO STAY
Heritance Kandalama Hotel Eco-property. Sigiriya, Dambulla; 94-66/555-5000; heritance hotels.com; doubles from **$$**.
WHAT TO DO
Golden Temple of Dambulla Five centuries-old carved and frescoed caves. Above the Colombo-Trincomalee road, Dambulla; 94-66/228-4760. **Peradeniya Botanic Gardens** The largest formal garden in Sri Lanka. Colombo-Kandy Rd., Peradeniya; 94-81/238-8238. **Polonnaruwa** 11th-century capital ruins. Polonnaruwa; 94-27/222-2121. **Sigirya** 560-foot-high rock, originally a king's fortress. Sigirya Project; 94-11/243-7059. **Temple of the Tooth** Buddhist temple with a golden roof. Palace Sq., Kandy; 94-81/2234-22226; sridaladamaligawa.org.

VIETNAM

WHERE TO STAY
Caravelle Hotel Centrally located, with an outdoor pool. 19 Lam Son Sq.; Ho Chi Minh City; 800/223-5652 or 84-8/823-4999; caravellehotel.com; doubles from **$$**. **De Syloia Hotel** Small and pretty, near the French Quarter. 17A Tran Hung Dao, Hanoi; 84-8/824-5346; desyloia.com; doubles from **$**. **Holiday View Hotel** Standard rooms near the beach. First of April Rd., Cat Ba Island; 84-313/887-200; doubles from **$**. **Sofitel Metropole** The grande dame of colonial hotels. 15 Ngo Quyen St., Hanoi; 800/763-4835 or 84-4/826-6919; sofitel.com; doubles from **$$**. **Victoria Can Tho Resort** Lovely riverside resort. Can Tho City, Mekong Delta; 84-71/810-111; victoriahotels-asia.com; doubles from **$$**.
WHERE TO SHOP
Le Minh Silk Tailor Specializes in locally made fabrics. 79–111 Hang Gai, Hanoi; 84-4/828-8728. **VIS Fashion** Trendy custom clothing. 16A Ly Nam De, Hanoi; 84-4/733-0933.
WHAT TO DO
Cat Ba National Park Emerald green water and spire-like limestone peaks. Ha Long Bay, Cat Ba Island; 840/313-888-761. **Quan Am Pagoda** One of the city's oldest, most elaborate temples. 12 D Lao Tu, Cho Lon; no phone.
TOUR OPERATORS
Handspan Adventure Travel Best for budget-oriented people. 84-4/926-0581; handspan.com; from $127 per person for a 2-day trip. **Trails of Indochina**

Custom itineraries with private guides. 84/844-1005; trailsofindochina.com; from $2,500 per person for a 10-day trip.

KUALA LUMPUR

WHERE TO STAY
Carcosa Seri Negara Thirteen suites in the former colonial governor's residence. Taman Tasik Perdana; 60-3/2295-0888; carcosa.com.my; doubles from **$$$**.
WHERE TO EAT
Senses Creations from chef Cheong Lieuw, originator of Asian fusion. Studio at Hilton Kuala Lumpur, 3 Jalan Stesen Sentral; 60-3/2264-2264; dinner for two ¶¶¶. **Third Floor Restaurant** Modern haute cuisine. JW Marriott Hotel Kuala Lumpur, 183 Jalan Bukit Bintang; 60-3/2141-3363; dinner for two ¶¶¶.
WHAT TO DO
National Mosque Modern, geometric building. 50480 Jalan Perdana; no phone. **Petronas Twin Towers** One of the biggest malls in Southeast Asia. Kuala Lumpur City Centre; petronastwintowers.com; no phone. **Sri Kandaswamy Kovil** Elaborate century-old temple. Brickfields; no phone.
NIGHTLIFE
Bar Ibiza Trendy dance club that attracts a 20-something crowd. 924 Jalan P. Ramlee; 60-3/2713-2233. **Royal Selangor Club** Private 123-year-old institution. Jalan Raja; 60-3/2692-7166. **Zouk** Multiple bars and nightly DJ's. 113 Jalan Ampang; 60-3/2171-1997.

⚿ **LODGING**   under $150 → **$** $150-$299 → **$$** $300-$699 → **$$$** $700-$999 → **$$$$** $1,000 + up → **$$$$$**

SINGAPORE

WHERE TO STAY

New Majestic Hotel Art-filled playpen for the party set. 31-37 Bukit Pasoh Rd.; 65-6/511-4700; newmajestichotel.com; doubles from **$$**. **The Scarlet** Sultry, plush boutique hotel. 33 Erskine Rd.; 65-6/511-3333; thescarlet.com; doubles from **$$**.

WHERE TO EAT

Graze Upmarket bistro and BBQ fare in grand colonial house-and-garden setting. 4 Rochester Park; 65-6/775-9000; dinner for two ¶¶¶.

WHERE TO SHOP

Asylum Concept store. 22 Ann Siang Rd.; 65-6/324-8264. **Front Row** Gourmet food plus fashion. 5 Ann Siang Rd.; 65-6/224-5502. **Style Nordic** Scandinavian clothing and housewares. 39 Ann Siang Rd.; 65-6/423-9114. **Vanilla Home** Interior design for the well-heeled. 48 Club St.; 65-6/324-6206.

WHAT TO DO

Clarke Quay Riverside strip of bars, clubs, and restaurants. 3 River Valley Rd.; 65-6/6337-3292. **Esplanade Theatres on the Bay** Landmark performing arts center. 1 Esplanade Dr.; 65-6/828-8222; esplanade.com.sg. **Supreme Court of Singapore** Futuristic building designed by Sir Norman Foster. 1 Supreme Court Lane; 65-6/336-0644.

NIGHTLIFE

Loof Bar Rooftop lounge surrounded by a neon-lit skyscape. 331 N. Bridge Rd., 03-07 Odeon Towers

Rooftop Extension; 65-6/338-8035. **Ministry of Sound** Dance club with hip-hop, disco, and electro-themed rooms. Block C, River Valley Rd., Clarke Quay; 65-6/235-2292.

BALI

WHERE TO STAY

Bulgari Resort 59 villas on an untouched beach. Jalan Goa Lempeh, Banjar Dinas Kangin, Uluwatu; 800/628-5427 or 62- 361/847-1000; bulgarihotels.com; doubles from **$$$$$**. **COMO Shambhala Estate** Recently revamped with a holistic spa. Begawan, Payangan Ubud; 62-361/ 978-888; cse.comoshambhala.bz; doubles from **$$**. **Four Seasons Resort Bali at Jimbaran Bay** 147 villas with thatched roofs and plunge pools. Denpasar; 800/332-3442 or 623-61/701-010; fourseasons.com; doubles from **$$$**. **Ubud Hanging Gardens** Dramatic river gorge setting. Desa Buahan, Ubud; 800/237-1236 or 62-361/982-700; ubudhanginggardens.com; doubles from **$$$**.

WHERE TO EAT

Ku De Ta Restaurant Bar Upscale Continental. 9 Lasmana Rd., Seminyak; 62-361/736-969; dinner for two ¶¶¶. **La Lucciola** One of the island's best restaurants, with a prime location. Oberoi Rd., Seminyak; 62-361/730-838; dinner for two ¶¶. **R. Aja's** Airy second-floor café. C13-15 Kuta Sq., Seminyak; 62-361/753-117; dinner for two ¶¶.

AUSTRALIA + NEW ZEALAND + THE SOUTH PACIFIC

BYRON BAY, AUSTRALIA

WHERE TO STAY

Byron at Byron Resort & Spa Balinese-style eco-resort in 45 acres of rainforest. 77-97 Broken Head Rd.; 61-2/6639-2000; thebyronatbyron.com.au; doubles from **$$$**. **Byron Bay Villa** 4-bedroom oceanfront rental. Watego's Beach; 61-2/9331-2881; contemporaryhotels.com.au; from **$$$$$** for a five-night stay. **Rae's On Watego's** Newly renovated hotel known for its restaurant. 8 Marine Parade; 61-2/6685-5366; raes.com.au; doubles from **$$$**.

WHAT TO DO

Belongil Bay Smooth seas, just west of town. **Cape Byron Lighthouse** Turn-of-the-20th-century structure with spectacular views. 61-2/6685-8807; byron-bay.com.

BLUE MOUNTAINS, AUSTRALIA

WHERE TO STAY

Lilianfels The best hotel in the mountains. Lilianfels Ave., Echo Point, Katoomba; 800/237-1236 or 61-2/4780-1200; lilianfels.com.au; doubles from **$$$**.

WHERE TO EAT

Apple Bar Excellent, crisp pizzas. 2488 Bells Line of Road, Bilpin; 61-2/4567-0335; lunch for two ¶¶¶.

Darleys Delicious local ingredients. Lilianfels Ave., Echo Point, Katoomba; 61-2/4780-1200; dinner for two ¶¶¶. **Lochiel House** Regional produce, Mediterranean influences. 1259 Bells Line of Road, Kurrajong Heights; 61-2/4567-7754; dinner for two ¶¶¶. **Solitary Restaurant & Solitary Kiosk** French-inspired menu. 90 Cliff Dr., Leura Falls; 61-2/4782-1164; dinner for two ¶¶¶. **Vulcan's** Specializes in braised meats. 33 Govetts Leap Rd., Blackheath; 61-2/4787-6899; dinner for two ¶¶¶¶.

WHAT TO DO

Blue Mountains National Park 85 miles of walking trails through blue forests, sandstone outcrops, and deep valleys. Great Western Highway, Katoomba; 61-2/4787-8877; nationalparks.nsw.gov.au. **La Maison du Livre** Cozy bookshop specializing in out-of-print titles. Shop 7, 166-168 The Mall, Leura; 61-2/4784-3360. **Mount Tomah Botanic Garden** The place to see the rare Wollemi pine. Bells Line of Road, via Bilpin; 61-2/4567-2154; bluemts.com.au. **Scenic World** Views of the World Heritage area from a glass-floored tram. Violet St. and Cliff Dr., Katoomba; 61-2/4782-2699; scenicworld.com.au.

MELBOURNE, AUSTRALIA

WHERE TO STAY

Hotel Causeway Business-traveler favorite in the center of the action. 275 Little Collins St., Melbourne; 61-3/9650-0688; causeway.com.au; doubles

Australia

● Byron Bay

—— Blue
Mountains

Melbourne ●

—— Bruny
Island

AUSTRALIA +
NEW ZEALAND +
THE SOUTH
PACIFIC

Fiji

Waiheke
Island

New Zealand

---

from **$$**. **Hotel Lindrum** Fantastic boutique property. 26 Flinders St., Melbourne; 61-3/9668-1111; hotel-lindrum.com.au; doubles from **$$$**.

WHERE TO DRINK

Abar Secret spot above a restaurant. 500 Chapel St.; 61-3/9826-3086. **Baraki Upo Mezethes** A fun bar housed in the Greek Orthodox Community Center. 168 Lonsdale St.; 61-3/9663-9971. **Double Happiness** Communist-themed décor. 21 Liverpool St.; 61-3/9650-4488. **Gin Palace** Excellent martinis. 10 Russell Place; 61-3/9654-0533. **Imbibe** Cocktails made with freshly squeezed juices. 653 Sydney Rd.; 61-3/9384-3040. **Manchuria** Moody, dimly lit, and Asian-inspired. First floor, 7 Waratah Place; 61-3/9963-1997. **Mango** Hip suburban bar. 17 Hall St.; 61-3/9372-8597. **Meyers Place** One of the original watering holes. 20 Meyers Place;

61-3/9650-8609. **Misty Place Bar** Frequented by budding art-world stars. 3-5 Hosier Lane; 61-3/9663-9202. **Robot** Shrine to Japanese pop culture. 12 Bligh Place; 61-3/9620-3646. **Tony Starr's Kitten Club** Modeled after a fifties diner, with jazz. Level 1, 267 Little Collins St.; 61-3/9650-2448. **The Undertaker** Potent drinks served in a former funeral parlor. 329 Burwood Rd.; 61-3/9818-3944.

BRUNY ISLAND, AUSTRALIA

WHERE TO STAY

Hiba Beach house with loft bedroom in a garden setting. 53 Adventure Bay Rd., Adventure Bay; 61-3/6293-1456; doubles from **$$**. **Inala** 2 private houses for rent on 500 acres. 320 Cloudy Bay Rd., Cloudy Bay; 61-3/6293-1217; inalabruny.com.au;

doubles from **$$**.

WHAT TO DO

Bruny Island Charters Excursions by boat along the island's coast. 915 Adventure Bay Rd., Adventure Bay; 61-3/6293-1465; brunycharters.com.au.

WAIHEKE ISLAND, NEW ZEALAND

WHERE TO STAY

Boat Shed Luxury B&B overlooking the bay. Tawa St. and Huia St., Oneroa; 64-9/372-3242; boatshed. co.nz; doubles from **$$$**.

WHERE TO EAT

Te Whau Vineyard Local produce and superb wines. 218 Te Whau Dr., Te Whau Peninsula; 64-9/372-7191; tewhau.co.nz; lunch for two .

WHAT TO DO

Goldwater Estate Excellent Bordeaux-style wine. 18 Causeway Rd., Putiki

Bay; 64-9/372-7493; gold waterestate.co.nz. **Passage Rock Wines** Try the Forte, the house specialty. 438 Orapiu Rd., RD1; 64-9/372-7257; passagerockwines. co.nz. **Rangihoua Estate** For olive-oil tastings. 1 Gordons Rd., Rocky Bay; 64-9/372-6214; rangihoua. co.nz. **Stonyridge** Amazing Cabernet blend. 80 Onetangi Rd., Onetangi; 64-9/372-8822; stonyridge.co.nz. **Waiheke Wine Centre** One-stop shop for locally produced bottles. 153 Oceanview Rd., Oneroa; 64-9/372-6139.

TRANSPORT

Fullers Ferries Regular 35-minute service from Auckland to Waiheke Island. 99 Quay St., Auckland; 64-3/9367-9111; fullers.co.nz. **SeaLink** Makes the 45-minute trip from Auckland's Half Moon Bay to Waiheke. 45 Jellicoe St., Freemans Bay, Auckland; 64-3/9300-5900; sealink.co.nz.

FIJI

WHERE TO STAY

Nukubati Island Private island resort with 14 solar-powered guest rooms. 800/707-3454 or 679/881-3901; nukubati.com; doubles from **$$$**, all-inclusive, with a 5-night minimum. **Royal Davui Resort** On an 8-acre speck of land. 310/928-1182 or 679/330-7090; royaldavui.com; doubles from **$$$$$**, including all meals. **Wakaya Club** Ultra-luxury private isle from the founder of FIJI water; 10 spectacular bungalows. 800/828-3454 or 679/344-8128; wakaya. com; doubles from **$$$$$**, all-inclusive, with a 5-night minimum.

INDEX

CONTRIBUTORS

Margaret Adair p. 18, from "Go Directly to College," Fall/Winter 2005 (T+L Family)

Mary Albon p. 194, from "Alexandria, Egypt," January 2007

Henry Alford p. 50, from "Scale a Volcano," September 2006; p. 53, from "Taking the High Road," July 2006

Gini Alhadeff p. 38, from "True West," April 2007; p. 116, from "The Other Side of Italy," July 2006

Richard Alleman p. 89, from "Bright Young Thing," October 2003

Tom Austin p. 29, from "Basel Dazzle," December 2006

Christene Barberich p. 45, from "LA Street," August 2006

Raul Barreneche p. 16, from "Critical Mass," March 2007; p. 48, from "Up at the Villa," February 2006; p. 57, from "Toronto's Time," April 2007; p. 140, from "Liepzig On View," July 2006

Laura Begley p. 70, from "New Wave Island Hopping," April 2006

Andrea Bennett, p. 78, "Bahamian Style"

Anya Von Bremzen p. 20, from "New York's Top 50," December 2006; p. 27, from "Table-Hopping in Atlanta," March 2007

Joan Juliet Buck p. 119, from "Ride Through Versailles," September 2006

Ian Buruma p. 128, from "Belgian Dreams," May 2006; p. 224, from "The End of the Earth," November 2006; p. 216, from "Manchurian Dreams," February 2006

Michael Caruso p. 200, from "Learn to be a Safari Ranger," September 2006

Paul Chai p. 254, from "Wishful Drinking," April 2006 (T+L Australia)

Ted Conover p. 91, from "Wild Things," September/October 2006 (T+L Family)

Christopher R. Cox p. 244, from "Bali's Future," November 2006

Linda Dannenberg p. 118, from "Best Boulangeries in Paris," February 2007; p.122, from "Great Bistros of Provence," May 2006

Meghan Daum p. 89, from "Lost Highway," February 2006

John Davidson p. 82, from "Mexico Magico," March 2007

Gregory Dicum p. 172, from "Getting Rila," May 2006

Simon Elegant p. 237, from "Back to the Future," August 2006

Amy Farley p. 36, from "Affordable Rockies," February 2007

James Fenton p. 143, from "A Tale of Two Cities," May 2006

Janet Franz p. 34, from "Chicago Heats Up," July 2006

Jonathan Gold p. 43, from "Disneyland: The Irreverent Guide," September/October 2006 (T+L Family)

Adam Goodheart p. 96, from "Fall Under the Spell of Easter Island," September 2006

Alice Gordon p. 67, from "Stacking the Decks," August 2006

Jaime Gross p. 42, from "Las Vegas for Less," March 2007; p. 49, from "Sonoma's New Star," July 2006

Dan Halpern p. 180, from "Beach Party," April 2006

James Patrick Herman p. 248, from "Making Waves Down Under," June 2006

Kendall Hill p. 240, from "Singapore Swings," September 2006 (T+L Australia)

Jennifer Howze p. 30, from "Austin, Texas," January 2001

Karrie Jacobs p. 220, from "Gambling on the Future," January 2007

George Kalogerakis p. 168, from "Aegean Odyssey," August 2006

David Kaufman p. 202, from "Tel Aviv Renaissance," March 2007; p. 73, "Colonial Caribbean"

David A. Keeps p. 136, from "Stockholm Syndrome," February 2007

Daniel Kurtz-Phelan p. 90, from "Colombia's New World," March 2007

Matt Lee and **Ted Lee** p. 55, from "Quebec: Past Perfect," February 2007; p. 146, from "Taste the Flavors of Piedmont," September 2006

Brad Leithauser p. 196, from "Africa Up Close," March 2006

Peter Jon Lindberg p. 136, from "Nordic Heights," May 2005

Nathan Lump p. 100, from "Patagonia Inside Out," November 2006

Charles MacLean p. 175, from "Montenegro," January 2006

Bruno Maddox p. 167, from "Tangerine Dreams," August 2005

Alexandra Marshall p. 73, from "The New Gold Coast," June 2006; p. 196, from "High Voltage Brazil," April 2007

Patricia Marx p. 105, from "A Skeptic's Spa Retreat," from October 2005

Connie McCabe p. 41, from "On the Chile Wine Trail," June 2006

Robert Milliken p. 257, from "Pure South Bruny Island," November 2006 (T+L Australia)

Pankaj Mishra p. 212, from "Inland Empire," February 2007

Clark Mitchell p. 138, from "Cologne," October 2006

Shane Mitchell p. 88, from "On the Tequila Trail," November 2006; p. 222, from "The Big Deep," March 2007; p. 261, from "A Distant Shore," October 2006; p. 86, from "The Best of Baja," November 2003

Kari Molvar p. 14, from "$250 a Day: Nantucket," April 2007

Alice Rawsthorn p. 110, from "All Eyes on London," May 2007

Sean Rocha p. 192, from "Visions of Cairo," December 2006

Max Rodenbeck p. 195, from "Capital Attraction," March 2006

Jeannie Ralston p. 30, from "Go Directly to College," Fall/Winter 2005 (T+L Family)

Julian Rubinstein p. 182, from "Riga is Ready," May 2007

Dana Sachs p. 234, from "Vietnam Now," Spring 2007 (T+L Family)

Guy Saddy p. 66, from "Making a Caribbean Hot Spot," January 2007

David Samuels p. 76, from "Grand Cayman Glitz," November 2006

Paul Schneider p. 14, from "The Best of Nantucket," April 2000

Bruce Schoenfeld p. 60, from "Okanagan Valley," October 2006; p. 176, from "Wine's Next Frontier," May 2006

Oliver Schwaner-Albright p. 31, from "Great American Architecture," November 2006

Maria Shollenbarger p. 126, from "Fleur de Lille," November 2006; p. 198, from "Welcome to Maputo," March 2007

Alex Shoumatoff p. 187, from "Pilgrimage to Russia," January 2007

Gary Shteyngart p. 102, from "Brazil's Untamed Heart," December 2006; p. 154, from "Hidden Rome," February 2007

Scott Spencer p. 164, from "Spanish Noir," May 2006

Valerie Stivers-Isakova p. 184, from "Russian Riviera," April 2007

Rima Suqi p. 24, from "Next Stop, Harlem," February 2007

Meeghan Truelove p. 26, from "Neighborhoods: Washington, D.C.," November 2006

Bonnie Tsui p. 219, from "Canton Revisited," November 2006

Sally Webb p. 251, from "The High Life," June 2006 (T+L Australia); p. 258, from "A Slice of Heaven," January/February 2006 (T+L Australia)

Susan Welsh p. 114, from "London's Borough Market," December 2006

Amy Wilentz p. 204, from "See the Future in Dubai," September 2006

Michael Z. Wise p. 19, from "A Modern Icon Steps Out," February 2007

Simon Worrall p. 115, from "Estate Planting," May 2006

Lynn Yaeger p. 132, from "Best of Barcelona," October 2006; p. 148, from "Head to the Source," September 2006

Most of these stories originally appeared in *Travel+Leisure* magazine, and have been updated and adapted for this book. To read the original stories or for more information about the destinations in this book, go to *travelandleisure.com*

In the lobby
of Dubai's Burj
Al Arab hotel.